D0984603

# Anchored in Love

## The Carter Family Story

MICHAEL ORGILL

# Anchored in Love

## The Carter Family Story

FLEMING H. REVELL COMPANY

*Old Tappan, New Jersey*

Scripture quotations in this book are from the King James Version of the Bible.

*Library of Congress Cataloging in Publication Data*

Orgill, Michael.
Anchored in love.

1. Carter Family. 2. Country music—United States—History and criticism. I. Title.
ML421.C3307 784'.092'2 [B] 75-12659
ISBN 0-8007-0735-4

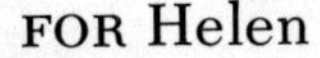
FOR Helen

# Contents

# Acknowledgments

I wish to thank Edward A. Kahn, without whose scholarship the history of early country music would be almost impossible to explore. Joe Bussard, a record collector with an intimate knowledge of the Carter Family, was of great help during the writing of this book.

Most importantly, I would like to thank Helen Orgill, and Minnie Orgill, who were of great help in the preparation of this book.

MICHAEL ORGILL

# Introduction

*Praise the Lord with harp: sing unto him with the psaltery and an instrument of ten strings.*
Psalms 33:2

In a time of historic events—July 1969—a strange juxtaposition of incidents occurred. The human race had visited the moon for the first time. Neil Armstrong and Buzz Aldrin were just about to bed down for the night. As one of their last duties, they radioed up to Michael Collins, the third crew member who was in orbit around the moon, to make sure a certain system was working. Collins turned on his microphone and began to quote figures to his crew mates. In the background, almost drowning out the static and the spoken figures, was a recording of Johnny Cash singing his classic "I Walk the Line." A musical form which had sprung from the most rural of origins was now coexisting in the most advanced technological environment the human race has ever known!

To those uninitiated into the world of country music this juxtaposition seemed bizarre, to say the least. In this case one would expect the music to correspond in some way with the sophisticated environment of a moon mission. It seemed inappropriate to have these heroes ride into space accompanied by country music. The music was primitive—it lacked the nobility which the occasion demanded. After all, wasn't the music of Tschaikovsky beamed to earth from Soviet orbital missions?

But to the country-music fan, as well as to others, it all was quite natural. The astronauts were highly intelligent scientists, but they were also middle-class Americans who shared a common culture with those who watched them on television. For these men, country music was simply a part of the natural order of things. It was as much a part of their world as the Tang they were supposed to drink. The music they enjoyed had come down the same road as the cultural processes which gave birth to their high level of achievement. Down the long road from farmer to extraterrestrial explorer, the music had been transformed from the melody of plow to the stuff of multimillion-dollar corporations.

For two centuries folk music was as far from the tenets of the marketplace as its players were from the expectation of monetary rewards. While the popular music of the cities became one forgettable song after another, folk music preserved its melodies and lyrics. A brief look at the origins of country music helps one to understand that it is not a monolithic entity.

Country music includes an aggregation of musical styles: the plaintive ballads of religious mountain folk, the work songs of the delta blacks, the spritely fiddle music of the Cajun, the Latin love songs of the Mexican in Texas, and the spirited music of the western cowboy among others. The differing styles were transformed to suit a theme or a purpose; the song idea could be a contemporary or historical tale, or an emotional expression. The technology of recording, and the subsequent development of radio and television brought these regional folk forms to a wider audience. Today we call these merged, commercialized musical forms "country music."

The sources of the music of the Carter Family were the folk and religious songs of the isolated, rural areas of the South. Since 1900 the word "hillbilly" had been used to denote the inhabitants of these southern Appalachian Mountain regions. But it was not until 1925 that the term was applied to the folk music of those hills. According to anthropologist Archie Green, an early recording session in New York brought new meaning to the word "hillbilly." Al and Joe Hopkins,

Tony Alderman, and John Rector traveled to the city from the southern hills to try their luck at the Okeh Record Company. An Okeh talent scout, Ralph Peer (who was later to play an important role in the career of the Carter Family) accepted them, and the group recorded six songs. After the session they asked Peer to find a name for their group. Al Hopkins, their leader, added that they were just a bunch of hillbillies from North Carolina and Virginia. As a result, Peer named the group "The Hillbillies."

The music they called "hillbilly" evolved out of the ballads and songs which the English and Irish immigrants brought to the southern mountain regions of this country. The music did not long remain apart from other influences—it drew material from many sources. The religious beliefs of the people also provided southern folk music with one source of style and content.

With the end of the American Revolution representatives of evangelical religious denominations began to travel throughout the Appalachian Mountains in search of converts and places to establish religious communities. The spiritually hungry folk of the wilderness were immediately attracted to this form of religion. The evangelical churches offered a sense of democracy, leaving these common people feeling they were wanted and needed in the religious life of the community. Furthermore, within a strictly defined system of morality, these denominations allowed the mountain folk to worship God as they wished.

Perhaps the greatest reason for the acceptance of these sects was their emphasis on singing in congregation. (The Methodists were known as "the singing church," for example.) People could be taught the precepts of the faith through the lyrics of religious hymns. Books, and the ability to read, were both rare on the frontier. Most songs were "lined"—the preacher would read the lyrics, two lines at a time, and the people would memorize them. This process allowed a wealth of song to be preserved over generations of southern Americans.

The doctrines of these churches were an important influence on the music. God was seen as an all-knowing, stern Being who threw souls into the fires of hell for their sins. He was also all-merciful. Any person who truly repented and asked for forgiveness would be saved from the hellfires. The Creator was seen as a force who kept a close watch on the activities of man. God was present at all times and in all places—no sinner could hope to escape His judgment. Life was a vale of tears, and only by obeying a watchful God could one continue to hope for a better world after this one.

Despite a desperate concern with the business of making a living, the mountain man consistently looked beyond this world to a reward in the next. When evils of society and unfairness of business interests oppressed him, he did not sing songs of protest (as his descendants, the hillbillies, were to do during the Depression). Instead, he looked to the world beyond the grave as the final solace. Songs, such as "This World Is Not My Home," are evidence of this great faith. Only the life everlasting would give recompense for the sufferings of this world.

The rural southerner, however, did not walk through the hills with the demeanor of a medieval monk. The struggle to wrest a living from the soil virtually required that one take a break, and release tensions with occasional escapes into revelry. Laughter and shouts of joy could be heard echoing over the valley at times. These other aspects of mountain life left their influence on the music, too.

No part of America has ever been totally isolated. Backwoods towns were visited by people from the outside world. Circuit riders brought news from the cities. Teachers came to live with families while teaching them to read. Itinerant peddlers from New England would brave the primitive mountain roads with their implement-laden carts. Occasionally these traders sold guitars or other instruments. There were traveling "medicine shows" touring the rural areas in brightly colored wagons; "tent repertoire" shows featuring magicians, acrobats, and other performers visited the smallest hamlets.

When elements of the rural population moved or traveled to the cities another source for songs joined the musical tradition. The young people, particularly, felt the pull of the city as a place to earn money, or an escape to adventure. There are hundreds of songs praising the life on the land, while others describe the loneliness of the poor country boy, lost amid the wiles and impersonal face of the city. The great railroad and trucking songs also come out of this tradition. Many a young farm boy lay awake at night listening to the mournful engine whistle and yearning for the hills of home.

The southern black was another influence on country musical form. The blues, honky tonk, jazz, work chants, and spirituals have all been adapted by the white southerner.

Everything the country singer heard was remembered and arranged into the folk style. This process preserved music which would have died out otherwise. The conservative South did not let songs die after a few months of incessant popularity. Songs sung years ago on Broadway (and forgotten) were being sung in the rural South.

The mountain music—called "hillbilly" in the mid-twenties—developed out of these diverse influences. It became part of a growing body of music which had a "country sound" and was essentially unknown to music lovers outside the South.

Two new technologies, recording and radio, made it possible to popularize this music beyond the regions where it developed. In the decades of the twenties and thirties a new group of entrepreneurs, spurred on by the commerical possibilities, found a rich harvest in that sound which then became known as "country music." The Carter Family, through early records and radio shows, would be among the first entertainers to bring their musical heritage—"country music"—to a wide audience.

# Anchored in Love

## The Carter Family Story

# 1

# Greater Riches

*. . . greater riches than the treasures in Egypt . . . .*

Hebrews 11:26

Maybelle Carter relaxed. The expectant and smiling faces of the audience at Bristol Auditorium calmed her. The people had been waiting for two hours. Johnny Cash's troupe encountered a delay at the airport, and had arrived for their engagement in Bristol, Virginia, one hour behind schedule. Maybelle always felt sorry about arriving late, because she thought of these people sitting in the darkness as friends. "If it weren't for them," A. P. Carter used to say, "I'd be selling fruit trees."

She felt concerned about the troupe's late arrival for another reason. It had all begun right here. Looking at the crowd she could see they knew as well. Country music still had a feeling of family about it, even though it was a tough, competitive business. You still sensed that the audience knew almost as much about you as you did yourself.

Not five blocks from the auditorium was a parking lot. On that site years ago there had been a music store. Its proprietor had told them, "The record-company man is coming through. Would you like to make a record? He's recording all the singers in these parts."

That Bristol recording session changed their lives. They had not realized it at the time, but it did happen. In a sense they became different people, though to the outward eye they hadn't changed at all. It all started at that moment when Ralph Peer, the record-company man, had pointed his finger at them in that fancy, big-city way of saying the recording machine had been turned on!

When the curtain rose, the audience produced a sudden wave of applause. It was as though they had been aching to clap their hands. They were there to hear Maybelle Carter sing. Maybelle looked to the side. To her right were Helen and Anita, two of her daughters. To the rear stood Carl Perkins and the Tennessee Three. Farther on to the right the Johnny Cash Singers were ready to begin the song. Johnny usually opened his shows alone, but he was letting Maybelle open with his sidemen. One singer was tapping the beat; and then, staying in the background, the group began humming in key. Maybelle touched the microphone lightly. This was the signal to begin. Maybelle struck the first chord on the Autoharp, and her daughters began to sing. The crowd knew the song at once, and their applause grew louder. "Keep on the Sunny Side" had been the Carter Family theme song.

She had known this song as long as she could remember, and on this night it sounded especially good. She saw the people in the front rows begin to nod their heads and rhythmically hit their hands against their knees. The Tennessee Three nodded their own appreciation and gradually faded back until the Carter Sisters were a world unto themselves—with only the slightest flick of brush against drum to back them up.

Whistles of approval came from the crowd as they wound up the song. On the last chord, the crowd broke into a thunderous applause again, but Maybelle knew it was only partly for her and her daughters. The crowd was anticipating the arrival of Johnny Cash and June Carter Cash.

It was always the way. Johnny and June were standing behind the curtain listening to the applause. The mayor of Bristol was MC and he was nervous. He coughed into the microphone. Maybelle sympathized with him. It had taken her several years before she could step out before more than twenty or thirty folks without feeling stage fright. She saw the mayor swallow briefly and move the microphone closer to his face. "Ladies and gentlemen," he began. Maybelle could barely hear his voice over the crowd. "Ladies and gentlemen! To make this homecoming complete, a great entertainer has come here to share our happiness at welcoming Maybelle Carter back again. I give you Mr. Johnny Cash!"

Cash moved slowly onto the stage, loping like a hungry, mountain wolf searching the sloping forests for prey. The Tennessee Three took up a slow beat, barely heard above the crowd. It reflected the way Johnny moved on stage. His guitar was mounted on his back and he was dressed in black. From Maybelle's line of sight, his high-heeled boots made him seem even taller than he really was. He is a large man and the spotlight barely caught all of him. People in the front rows rushed the stage, and Johnny stepped toward the edge. He shook hands with a few of them before stepping back and taking the guitar off his back. He raised it over his head briefly before adjusting the straps that rested against his chest.

Hundreds of flashbulbs flashed and Maybelle blinked her eyes. The Tennessee Three kept the rhythm going until the crowd stepped back from the stage. As soon as the crowd became expectantly silent, Johnny struck a chord and began. The song was "I Walk the Line." The cheers and whistles were louder when he finished. He waved at the crowd and sang

"Folsom Prison Blues." The crowd roared again, and he sang another, and another. They were totally with him. They smiled and nodded with almost every phrase he sang.

Now Maybelle saw her daughter June rush out across the stage, a microphone in her hand. She is a beautiful woman, Maybelle thought. She moved with a bouncy assurance across the stage to Johnny's side. He sang the first line of their hit "Jackson"; the audience knew it instantly and greeted it with a roar. June brought the microphone up and answered him. Maybelle knew the crowd saw them as the perfect example of a man and woman in love. She grinned when June got more and more involved in the song and responded to Johnny in a fighting tone. They were two lovebirds sparring with each other, and the audience loved it!

Johnny grinned a lopsided grin, giving out a sharp, high shout. Maybelle Carter saw the love in his eyes for her daughter. Suddenly all nervousness left her, and she felt as if she were performing in the parlor of her Nashville home with many good friends for her audience. It was as if these were people who happened to be passing when the family was singing and playing in the living room. Tears swam in her eyes, and her vision blurred. Johnny motioned to her, asking her to join them at center stage. The audience understood his gesture immediately and let out a whoop. She looked out at them for a moment. The people nodded and looked into each other's eyes, and they were smiling, laughing, and applauding.

Maybelle cradled her Autoharp and joined them before the microphone. There was a catch in her throat. Life had come full circle through all the happiness and all the sorrow, through a world war, and through personal setbacks. She had been lucky.

Restraining the tears welling up in her eyes, she saw Johnny give them a smiling cue to begin, and she strummed the first chords on the Autoharp. June's clear voice sang out with the opening lines of "Ring of Fire." Maybelle came in with the harmony, strumming her chords. Johnny backed it all up with his firm, low voice which held the same quiet strength A. P. Carter had always possessed. The crowd murmured as they continued to harmonize. Maybelle, June, and Johnny wove a spell, drawing images and memories out of the past. It was as if the audience saw with her own eyes, as if the first Carter Family were standing on the stage—not Johnny and June Cash with Maybelle Addington Carter.

They ended the song and the curtain closed for the first intermission. A line from the Bible came into Maybelle's thoughts as the musicians filed off stage. . . . *greater riches than the treasures of Egypt.* . . . She had heard that line from Hebrews used in a song thirty or so years ago in the Clinch

Mountains. It was sung by a withered old gentleman sitting on the porch of the Gate City General Store.

Didn't that line apply to her? Maybelle felt her life to be a vessel filled to overflowing, and she could not understand why such good fortune should, in the end, be with her. Perhaps it was the roots she had in the country for miles around the Bristol Auditorium. She had sung ever since she could remember, even before she learned how to read. By the age of ten she could play the guitar, the fiddle, and the Autoharp. (All of this was self-taught and on borrowed instruments.) Perhaps it was because she had always followed the kind of life that God and His Word had seemed to lay out for her. She had followed this life in the best way she could.

Yes, she felt especially blessed. . . . *greater riches than the treasures of Egypt.* . . . Maybelle Carter's mind drifted back to the mountains surrounding Maces Spring, Virginia. That's where it all began.

2

# A Good Land

*. . . a good land and a large . . . a land flowing with milk and honey . . . .*

Exodus 3:8

Visit Scott County, Virginia, on a sweltering summer day—just as the afternoon sun is touching the peaks of the Clinch Mountains. Wander down the daisy-bordered country road. There are only a few farm houses and none of them looks inhabited. Walk into an overgrown front yard and you feel the air of abandonment around the weathered hulk of the house. You are sure no one is still trying to carry on a living here. Call out a greeting to make sure, but your shout just echoes down through the valley.

There's another farm house within sight—gaping hole in the roof, a splintered roof beam jutting out. There's little prospect of habitation there either.

This is Carter country, although little is really known about the family. Maybe you do have an old pamphlet, printed by A. P. Carter, entitled "Bible Questions and Answers." (You know the Carter Family music group found its first audiences in the local churches.) And you know this "seed" group was present when country music began—and it all started in these hills.

The Bible says, "A branch shall grow out of his roots. . . ."(*See* Isaiah 11:1.) And these are the roots of this remarkable family: Clinch Mountains, Wise and Scott Counties, Maces Spring, Gate City (the county seat of Scott County)—all are associated with the legend of the Carter Family. Driving through these country roads brings the names alive for you. Feel the concrete and macadam of a mountain grade gently give way to a descent into a shaded and fertile valley. Hum some of the Carter Family tunes. Associate the music in your mind with this magnificent and hospitable countryside.

If you are a city person, though, you may look at it all with a different perspective. This land of hills, covered with carpets of green, is certainly lovely; however, it has been anything but hospitable to the residents of these counties. It is a land which has always demanded the utmost in work and dedication from its inhabitants. It was here, in this "good land and large," that the

Carter family lived and were to set their musical roots. Scott County was their home until they began the performing and recording career which catapulted them to international fame. It was here that A. P. Carter died. The family returned again and again to these beloved hills for spiritual renewal.

The music of the Carters was influenced by their environment to a greater degree, perhaps, than is the music of most performing artists today. Contemporary performers have many sources of inspiration available to them. Music is carried over international boundaries by mass media. Artists and performers are initially influenced by their culture. As they develop, the mores and styles of other cultures intrude into their consciousness; their personal styles and messages are inevitably molded in ways which might be entirely foreign to their background. The Carter Family participated in this century's initial expansion of the entertainment media, but their music was not formed by it. Their art was the product of an essentially self-contained and self-nurturing tradition. For them, the cradle of this tradition was their native Clinch Mountains.

It would be wrong to say that Scott County was typical of the South, or even typical of Virginia. Viewing the South as a monolithic region is inaccurate and misleading. Scott County is located in the southwestern section of Virginia and borders on the state of Tennessee. It is entirely within the Appalachian

Mountains, a major chain of picturesque, green elevations extending through the eastern United States into Canada. This county has more in common with the other mountainous regions of Virginia, Tennessee, Kentucky, West Virginia, and North Carolina than it has with the rest of the state of Virginia. Scott County is bisected by a local range, the Clinch Mountains, and the land is uneven—a texture of steep hills, and shaded, deep valleys. The most common geographical feature in Scott County is a series of confined, narrow valleys, cut off from one another by smaller mountains, hills, and ridges. When not overworked the soil is productive, and the land boasts a good water supply fed by springs, streams, and rivers.

The quietude of these hills and valleys is misleading, however. Money was always hard to come by in Scott County. According to the Bureau of Population and Economic Research of Virginia, in 1940 the average annual income was a paltry two hundred dollars. Even taking into account a standard of living which de-emphasized money as a necessity, this figure is astonishingly low, and speaks volumes about the poverty and isolation of most folks in Scott County at that time.

The lack of money, and the calm, isolated life imposed by the seemingly eternal presence of the sheltering hills, enforced an essentially bartering economy upon the people of the county. Tobacco was the only real cash crop, being especially suitable for cultivation on small plots of ground. The people of the Clinch

Mountains also grew apples, peaches, hemp, oats, and some other grains. Most small farmers also had some hogs and cows, as well as horses. Some had large orchards, and prepared their products for sale by preserving the fruit in drying houses.

The coming of the railroads broke Scott County's almost total isolation from the rest of the United States. The economic life of the area was vitalized, and goods and money began to move more rapidly in and out of the county. When the railroads were built the highways were also developed. There was a need to carry heavy loads in wagons and other types of vehicles which could not traverse the foot and horse trails of earlier days. But it was not until much later that automobile roads were paved in the area.

In 1915 most people in the county lived on farms. They tilled the soil to raise the crops they needed to feed themselves, but there was little or no surplus to sell for profit. These were isolated people, whose farmhouses served as the center of the only world they would ever know. Their social lives were very limited when compared to the ways of the city. There were almost no telephones, mail came two or three times a week, and month-old newspapers were commonplace.

However, the people had deep religious convictions to sustain them. Their Christian beliefs were most of all expressed through their music, an art form their ancestors had brought over the sea. They sustained and renewed their faith through the generations.

To an outsider life here might seem hard indeed. But to these people, theirs was “a good land and a large,” which their faith and music enriched and ennobled. That very faith, and that music were part of a larger story which went far beyond the boundaries of Scott County. In this region people kept and nurtured their native culture and traditions—refining and purifying them to the point where the soul-penetrating power of their music would influence and sweep the mass culture of America.

# 3

# Grace Unto the Humble

*. . . God resisteth the proud, but giveth grace unto the humble.*

James 4:6

Travel through Bristol, Virginia, and cross over into the Tennessee section of this border town. Traffic rumbles along State Street and the inhabitants, preoccupied with their own affairs, pass up and down as if it were like any other street in America. But for the country-music fan, there is a sense of the history of the place. On State Street there is a car-filled parking lot at the site where the Carter Family trio, Sarah, Maybelle, and A.P., made their first recording for Ralph Peer. Time is a spendthrift; there is no commemorative plaque or other sign to show that, in 1929, musical history had been made here. Instant America buries its history under pavements and parking meters. The Carters were fortunate; many who had never heard their names were in their debt. Their legacy lived on in the musical subconscious of America; that was better than any bronze plaque!

Return to Virginia and drive to the west to Gate City, county seat of Scott County. In the country, a dozen miles outside of Gate City, lives Virgie Carter Hobbs—a genuinely friendly, white-haired woman who is a sister of A.P. She is reputed to be the family historian, but would be the first to say that Maybelle could tell more about the family's music career than she, herself, can. There are different kinds of questions, though—like those about the Carters' lives before the beginning of their country-music careers—that this warm and likeable woman can answer. A careful search turned up very little information about A. P. Carter's background, but Virgie Hobbs, being his sister, would know as well as anybody. An open, good-humored woman, she is willing to talk about her family and the brother they nicknamed Doc.

There was deep snow on the ground the cold night when A. P. Carter was born. The vine-covered Carter family homestead, nestled in Little Valley between Hiltons and Maces Spring, was ablaze with the light of kerosene lamps. The Carters were more than a mile away from their closest neighbor, but those with houses on the hillsides could have seen the light spilling out over the snow. They must have wondered. It was the night of December 15, 1891.

The delivery was difficult. It was the first child of Robert C. Carter and Mollie Arvelle Bays Carter, and two midwives had been in the house since sunset. Mollie Arvelle was a brave woman, but this baby had worried her even before the labor pains started. She had visited her mother three months before, in early September. She had ridden up the narrow mountain path, sitting sidesaddle on the family quarter horse. It was a lovely day when she started out, but the sky darkened as she rode up the mountain slope, and by the time she arrived at her mother's house, flashes of lightning were coursing through the clouds. There was a river a quarter of a mile from her mother's front porch, and it had begun to run over its banks.

Mollie Arvelle Carter spent the entire visit huddling with her mother in the kitchen. A terrific thunderstorm exploded around them. It lasted for hours, and it was a mountain belief that violent weather had effects on children in the womb. Mollie Carter had been worrying ever since the thunderstorm. It troubled her, especially during the final months when she was unable to help her husband with the winter chores. She sat in the snug log cabin and watched through the window as he chopped the winter wood.

The difficult delivery confirmed her fears. At first,

only one midwife had been called, a second cousin from Hiltons Spring; but before the evening's darkness had become total, Robert Carter was forced to ride on the quarter horse toward Maces Spring to bring another. They returned just in time, shortly before midnight. In short order A.P.'s squeals filled the cabin. Mollie Carter's pain was eased by the look on her husband's face when one of the midwives held the red baby upside down, high in the air, and slapped its bottom. The baby's wails began, and a broad smile spread across Bob Carter's face.

She might, at that moment, have thought back to the night she met him. Mollie Arvelle Bays had been working hard for a week, helping her mother and several of the neighbor women with a quilt. All the women around who belonged to the Friendly Grove Methodist Church gathered once a week to stretch a half-finished quilt over a table. Together they would sew new scraps of cloth and increase its size. When it was finished, they would sell it at a fair to raise money for the church.

There had not been a square dance in the neighborhood for months, and even though Mollie's father was extremely religious and had objections to fiddle music and dancing, her mother winked when she discovered Mollie's plans. After promising to be home at a decent hour, she walked at dusk to the large barn where the fiddlers had already started to play.

Mollie could not count the blazing kerosene lamps which lit the inside of the barn. Four large barrels had been rolled into the back of the building, and a stage of planks had been erected on top of them. A string band was playing loudly and the men were tapping their feet to the music.

Life in Little Valley was a constant struggle, and most families worked all the year around to keep food on the table. The soil was thankless. God rewarded those who accepted that fact about His world, and still worked His land with a joyous heart. Rewards were to be found beyond this world in the glorious home He prepares there for the righteous. Unlike the modern American, who looks toward tomorrow for the fulfillment of his material desires, the residents of Little Valley knew tomorrow would be no better than today. So they cultivated a serious attitude toward life, and tried to steer clear of frivolous activity.

But man is a playing animal, no matter how strenuously he might work to suppress this side of his nature. There had been heavy rains in Scott County during the months before the barn dance, and the skies had seemed always covered with clouds. Suddenly, just about the time when Mollie and the women finished the quilt, the sun had broken through and shined down on the hills and valleys. It was as though a burden had been lifted from their hearts, and they could not restrain themselves. A barn dance was the thing to have, and they would have to have it now, before the fall came, and they were once again plunged into feverish preparations for the coming of winter.

Hay was swept off the floors of the barn and stuffed into the storage places in the walls. Dancers filled the clean barn floor, and the fiddle music rang out. It was as though they were all dancing in a building made of hay. Mollie danced for a while with a few of the young men she knew from the brief time she had spent in the schoolhouse. When she became tired, she went over to the punch table where a jolly farmer she vaguely knew offered her some punch mixed with moonshine. She smiled, declined, and drank some fruit juice instead. There was no end to the jokes and teasing. It was as though everybody saved up their humor for the barn dance, letting it loose all at once in an explosion of laughter.

Her drink in hand, she pushed through the crowd lining the sides of the dance floor. Mollie Arvelle Bays wanted a closer look at the string band. They were just picking up speed, playing the fastest dance tunes they knew, and Mollie wanted to see if she knew any of the musicians. Abruptly, as she edged up to the corner of the stage, the fiddle player stopped playing and stared at her. The rest of the band trailed off, surprised at the fiddle's sudden dropping away. Mollie turned her eyes away from the man. She could feel a sudden blush spreading through her cheeks.

"There now boys, play without me for a while," the fiddler said, and came over to sit on the edge of the stage next to the spot where Mollie was standing. The band, now composed of two guitars and a mouth harp, struck up the song again; the fiddler jumped down to the floor and took Mollie's hand, leading her out to the dance floor.

As they danced, she noticed the man's shoes. He wore blue, patent-leather boots with high tops, and the highest heels Mollie had ever seen. The fiddler was an excellent dancer, and as the two of them went through their paces, the other revelers stopped whatever they were doing and stood on the sidelines to watch. When they were finally the only couple dancing, Mollie had to stop in embarrassment.

A sound of laughter came from the bandstand, and everybody else followed the musician's lead, guffawing in good-natured fun at Mollie's embarrassment. The fiddler stood with his arms akimbo, grinning broadly. He seemed to Mollie at that moment the best-dressed young man at the dance. He wore a new, red-plaid, wool shirt. Blue-striped, white trousers were tucked into the tops of his boots.

Mollie was later to tell her children, "Your father was the prettiest man I had ever seen dance." When he went back to rejoin the string band his fiddle playing impressed her, even though she came from a family which regarded stringed instruments as "works of the devil."

Later during one of the breaks, Bob told her he had recently completed a trip from Indiana. Virgie Hobbs would recall that her mother had never met anyone who had traveled so far away from Scott County. Bob

Carter had been working in several Indiana railroad yards as a laborer, sending money home to his parents, and he told Mollie of his hopes of getting a job with the railroad in Roanoke.

From that day forward, Mollie Arvelle Bays was in love. But all was not to go smoothly. Mollie's father, an elder of the Friendly Grove Methodist Church, and her mother had reared five God-fearing children. Although Bob Carter was unknown to Mollie, her father had heard of him, and there were objections to her seeing a worldly, fiddle-playing fellow.

Bob Carter returned Mollie's affection. When her father took him aside on the day he asked for Mollie's hand, Bob promised that, after the wedding day, he would forever lay the fiddle and the bottle aside. Mollie's father was mollified by this promise. After the wedding in December 1889, he brought his minister over to Bob and Mollie's cabin many times; in due course, Bob was converted and saved. He accepted Jesus Christ as his personal Saviour and he refrained from drinking and playing the fiddle for the rest of his life.

Music, however, was an integral part of mountain life, and Bob Carter never lost his love for the old ballads. He continued to sing them and in later years avidly followed the careers of A.P. and the rest of the family.

Two years after they were married, Mollie gave birth to their first child. They named him Alvin Pleasant, after a man Bob had worked for in the railroad yards of

Indiana. Eventually Bob and Mollie would rear eight children.

Bob Carter's conversion was not a frivolous decision. The Carter children were all raised in an intensely religious atmosphere. Paradoxically, this religiosity was most expressed through the medium of religious ballads and hymns, which both Bob and Mollie taught their children. The work around the Carter homestead in those days was constant, and there was little time for frivolity. But when the family could get together on the porch on a cool, summer evening, or by the stove on a snow-swept, winter night, they passed the time making music.

Mollie Bays Carter was the main repository of the religious music in the household. She taught her children such songs as "Sailor Boy," "Brave Soldier," and "Wife of Usher's Well," singing them in a high, quavering soprano. At night, when the sound travels well in the hills, passersby would stop by the road and listen to her sing.

As the years went by, the old Carter homestead became steeped in the musical lore of the hills. The two streams of mountain experience—religion, and the harshness of making a living in this world—both led into a single musical expression. As he grew older, Bob Carter's religious faith intensified and his love for music increased. His offspring inherited this talent for music.

When he was seven or eight years old, A.P. tried his hand at the fiddle. His mother had instructed him to carry a bucket of coals over the mountain trail into Hiltons. There he was to give them to Flanders Bays, his mother's brother. Just as he arrived at the Bays's cabin, a sudden rainstorm erupted. Young A.P. was forced to take shelter with his uncle until the storm passed.

During the rainstorm Flanders Bays taught A.P. some rudimentary chords on the fiddle. It was the first time the young boy had ever held an instrument in his hands. He must have had mixed feelings, since he had always been taught that stringed instruments were the tools of the devil. But his uncle had put the fiddle in his hands, and A.P.'s love of music was too strong for him to refuse. In the weeks and months which followed A.P. would often travel the paths to the Bays's cabin. There he was taught how to sing harmony, the reading of shape notes (a method of reading music by paying attention to the special shapes of the notes), as well as further fingerings on the fiddle.

During the whole of A.P.'s early life, Flanders Bays played an important part in the boy's musical education. Mr. Bays later conducted a choir at the Friendly Grove Methodist Church in which A.P. sang bass. Learning of the boy's intense interest in music, Mollie Carter taught her son all the religious songs she knew, and Bob Carter sang to the boy all the ballads he had learned in his travels from Scott County to Indiana.

A.P.'s father winked at his son's interest in the fiddle.

Bob Carter had made his peace with God, but in his heart he must have believed one could play the fiddle and still serve the Lord. But he wisely kept A.P.'s new skill from Mollie Bays Carter.

Other children were also tempted by the "devil's instrument." One summer night, when it was too hot for E. J. Carter (Maybelle's future husband) to sleep in the house, he rested outside near the tobacco patch. While he snored, his mother, wondering where E.J. was keeping himself, sneaked up to the outside sleeping area. While E.J. slept soundly, she discovered an old fiddle hidden under the straw. Mollie Carter threw it down the hill, woke the boy up, and gave him a sound licking.

A.P.'s brother Jim tried his hand at the five-string banjo, keeping it from his mother, of course. Sylvia, the youngest of the children, became quite a good guitar player, and in later years often played with the Carter Family when they went on tour. Grant, one of the other brothers, also took up the fiddle, playing with the Family during their personal appearances.

Virgie Carter Hobbs never learned to play any stringed instruments, but her interest in the mountain musical tradition was strong. In the years since 1915 she taught A.P. and the group mountain tunes and ballads she had picked up in her travels around Scott and Wise Counties.

A.P.'s early life was excellent preparation for his future career. Because of their religious convictions,

Mollie and Bob Carter raised a family steeped in the music of their environment. But while Alvin Pleasant Carter loved and practiced the music of his people, there was no thought that one could make a living from it. A musical career was out of their realm of experience and was simply never considered. A.P. reached manhood with only one imperative. He must begin to make money for the Carter homestead.

One morning in the early spring of 1910 A.P.'s father met him on the path leading from the Maces Spring school to the Carter cabin. (In the mountains schooling was sporadic, and young people often continued to attend school well into their early adulthood.) Together they sat on a fallen log. Bob Carter told his son that new problems had suddenly beset the family. The Carters had been unable to pay their county taxes in the past year as bad weather had caused their only cash crop, tobacco, to fail. Many families in the area were also unable to come up with their tax money, and the tax collectors had begun to get tough. Unless the Carters began to make payments they would lose their homestead.

He would look for a job himself, Bob Carter continued, but right now there was much work to be done getting the tobacco crop started for the year, and there was other work around the cabin that always needed doing. Having helped his father throughout his life, A.P. knew this. Besides, Mollie was with child again

—the baby they would christen Sylvia when she was born—and Bob Carter felt he had to remain behind in Scott County. It was only then that A.P. fully realized what his father was saying.

Three days later he quit school and traveled with his brother Jim, on horseback, to Bristol. From there he took the first train ride of his life to Cincinnati, Ohio, where he caught another train to Indianapolis. His father had given him the addresses of several people he had known when he had worked in Indiana, and A.P. hoped they would tell him where to find work.

Neither Bob Carter nor his son knew of the business slowdown which had hit Indianapolis months before A.P. left Scott County. The railroad yards were not hiring. The names his father had given him were not known. They must have moved away since Bob Carter last worked in the area.

A.P. was forced to earn his room and board at the Salvation Army by washing dishes and sweeping floors. The people at the mission were very kind to him, but they could offer him little hope. Jobs were scarce, and even if he found one, it probably would not be anything steady.

A.P. searched for two weeks before landing a week's work as a day laborer for the city of Indianapolis. He spent the time digging ditches for a new sewer system on the outskirts of the city. He demonstrated that he was a willing worker. The foreman took a liking to him and convinced the city to hire A.P. full-time. For the first time, since leaving Scott County, he felt some hope.

A.P. returned to the Salvation Army mission the night he was given a permanent job and paid the astonished manager a month's room and board in advance. The work was hard and long, but he applied himself, and did his uncomplaining best. Every cent he had left, after paying room and board, was mailed home weekly to the Carter homestead in Scott County.

Alvin Pleasant missed the hills and valleys of his native county. Lying on his bunk in the Salvation Army dormitory, he began to compose his first songs. Using mountain tunes he knew by heart, he wrote new lyrics, expressing his profound loneliness for the people and countryside he loved. He wrote the words on the backs of used envelopes which the workers in the mission gave him, and stuffed them in with the money he was sending back home. The lyrics flowed out of him. They were his first songs, and they came directly from his experience. The Carter Family's theme song, "Keep on the Sunny Side," dates back to this period. More than twenty years before the Carter Family came together A.P. wrote the first version of the song which would identify them to millions of people around the world.

It was quite difficult for Alvin Pleasant Carter in Indianapolis. Even though he had a steady job, his room and board ate up three-fourths of his weekly wage, and the amount he was sending home was far less than his father had expected.

The worry and anxiety A.P. must have experienced were eased by the religious faith he had inherited from his parents. One could not expect favors or any easy time from *this* life. Life is harsh; nothing more was expected.

"Keep on the Sunny Side" is often dismissed by sophisticated, contemporary listeners as pure Pollyanaism. It seems too simple to declare that all will be well, if we just keep looking at the sunny side of life. This viewpoint ignores certain facts about A. P. Carter's environment and beliefs. This world, as A.P. saw it, is only a secondary adjunct to heaven. The "sunny side" of the song is not found here in this world, for the most part. In the midst of the worst trouble or loneliness, one looks beyond the facts of *this* life, and sends the soul aspiring toward the *mercy* of the Lord. The "sunny side" is the *light of God's Wisdom.*

A.P. knew the ways of loneliness. In the mountains thousands had sung of it. As the Book of Proverbs has it, "As a bird that wandereth from her nest, so is a man that wandereth from his place" (27:8). The mountain people were so attached to their countryside that enforced separation was hard on them. A.P. knew the truth in these songs—that a man can wane away physically when he is too long gone from home.

The young man began to feel his health slip away.

Winter swept over Indianapolis, and A.P. was getting more colds than he had ever had before. Bad weather held up the construction crews; snow swirled into half-dug ditches, and ice-coated girders were bare sticks against a gray sky. He was forced to wash dishes and sweep floors at the mission for his room and board. Since he had no income, no money was being sent back to Scott County.

In February he was struck down by typhoid fever. The mission workers tended him, as they did others who were victims of a small epidemic now sweeping the city. He remained in the dormitory for two or three weeks before he felt well enough to board a train for home. He used the other half of the round-trip ticket which he had bought when he began his trip north.

A.P. had to lay over in Cincinnati when the fever flared up, but he stayed there only a few days. The Cincinnati Salvation Army mission helped him to get a medical examination. He had recovered almost entirely from the typhoid, but simply needed a few days to rest.

Two weeks after leaving Indianapolis he arrived at Bristol in late afternoon and hitched a ride back to his home on an empty hay wagon. He came up to the cabin at night, and the kerosene lamps hanging on the porch were the only lights he could see. Bob and Mollie Carter welcomed him back with hardly a word about his unexpected arrival. They brought him into the kitchen. A.P. assured them he had regained his health, and they talked about Indiana until their conversation slowed gradually into silence. After a supper of pork and beans, he sang a few songs with his parents and those of his brothers and sisters who were old enough to be awake.

In Indianapolis, music had been his insulation against the long, cold nights. *How shall we sing the Lord's song in a strange land?* The line from Psalms (137:4) might have occurred to him while he was alone and lonely in Indianapolis. Back in Maces Spring it was quickly becoming easy to sing again.

# 4

# Walking Toward the Lord

*As ye have therefore received Christ Jesus the Lord, so walk ye in him.*

Colossians 2:6

After A. P. Carter recovered from his bout with typhoid, he returned to school. Even though he had just turned twenty, A.P. still had six months of schooling to finish. The educational system of Scott County was designed to provide only what the mountain dweller needed for his life in the country, the proverbial readin', writin', n' 'rithmetic. Neither of his parents had managed to finish what little schooling was available in Scott County. They were anxious that their firstborn son should get his education. Despite his protests that he could make more money for the family by staying at home, A.P. was sent to the school in Maces Spring for two hours a day.

Alvin Pleasant Carter was never to finish his schooling. The one-room schoolhouse closed after only two months. (The gabble of his classmates, the oldest of whom was five years his junior, annoyed him long before that.) The school quite simply ran out of money. There was nobody in Scott County who could continue to pay the bills. Released from school in midsummer, A.P. immediately set out to earn some money and help his family.

He scoured the neighborhood, but there were few, if any, immediate jobs which would earn him cash within the confines of Scott County. He was finally forced to travel again, but this time he did not have to go far. A.P. went to nearby Dickinson County, where he had heard the opportunities were better.

There he met the owner of a small nursery who was just setting up his business. A.P. was offered a job selling fruit trees to farmers throughout the area. The nurseryman claimed the trees would sell quickly. He loaned A.P. a good horse, and the young man was in business. He rode every horse path in Dickinson, Wise, and Scott Counties and he got to know everybody very well. "People want cash money," the nurseryman had said. A.P. readily agreed as he had the same need himself. The man claimed the farmers would buy as fruit crops were still in demand and could be sold for cash. A.P. could see nothing wrong with that argument.

Unfortunately, the farmers could see the other side of the situation. Cash money was scarce, and there was even less of it available for fruit trees—whatever future income they might provide. A.P. hawked his trees everywhere and met with only limited success. Alvin Pleasant was quite likeable and made friends easily. Some of these were lucky enough to have money and they would buy a tree from him. In this way he made a little cash and gave most of it to his parents. But all was not easy for him. In the course of his first full-time job A.P. fell into some habits he was later to regret.

He did not fall into womanizing, as some of his friends had done. He respected women too much for that. Drinking was what tempted him most and this temptation, ironically, was linked to his musical talent. It seemed a harmless thing at first.

After the long days of traveling around the county, he would gather with some friends to sing music at a local tavern in Maces Spring. (This was what passed for urban life in Scott County.) A.P. was a young man trying out his wings. The temptations common to his place and time confronted him; he responded in the same ways as others had before him. It became easier and easier to take a drink when the music was flowing freely and all the boys wanted to stay for just one more song before heading homeward. An unsuccessful day spent selling trees was tiring and frustrating—drink helped take the edge off of weariness. After he became accustomed to the taste of it (it utterly revolted him at first), he seemed to play and sing better.

His drinking problem became serious after A.P. joined a "physick" show. The medicine show operator, traveling in a multicolored wagon, rolled into town under the cover of night. Sometimes, in the more religious parts of the South, it was best for the operator not to enter a town flamboyantly. It was more tactful to camp at a strategic crossroads and greet the people in the morning—with the sales pitch and the music already going full blast. It seemed to offend their morals less; and, with a crowd already gathered about the wagon, it was more difficult for the local constable to kick a "physick" show out of town.

A.P. was walking home when he saw it. He made a mental note to come back to Maces Spring after his rounds the next day. The "physick" shows often had good musicians who toured around the country with them, and he hoped to learn something from these professional musicians.

When A.P. rode into Maces Spring the next day he saw a crowd gathered around the wagon. He could hear the voice of the medicine man over the subdued murmur of the people. "Friends," the spiel went, "I come here with new discoveries. The last time we gathered together I could offer you no solace from the gout, but the finest medical minds of Europe. . . ." It ran on and on in a smooth, lulling patter. A.P. was impatient as he tied up his horse and made sure the fruit trees were securely tied down on the wagon. The medicine man held up bottles of various shapes, each with its own multicolored label. There were bottles for the common cold, gout, dropsy, ulcers, tumors, canker sores, coughs, heart trouble, and almost any ailment likely to strike down a human being. For the most part, the people kept their hands in their pockets, and the medicine man's face gradually took on a desperate look. The crowd was falling out of his grasp.

A.P. walked over to the edge of the crowd. Several friends called out to him to get up on the end of the wagon and sing. It seemed the "physick" show was second-rate—it had no touring entertainers. A crowd without much cash could not be expected to part with any of it, unless there was some music to sweeten the idea. Others urged A.P. on, and his friends offered to play with him. He did not have an instrument, but he could sing bass. Two other men, friends at the tavern, were pushed up on the back of the wagon by the crowd. One man played guitar, the other one played the mouth harp, and both sang tenor.

As twilight gathered, the three men sang ballads and sacred songs, and the crowd increased. After an hour, when darkness was forcing the crowd to disperse, the medicine man folded up his wagon. He had sold more patent medicines than he had expected. He took A.P. aside and offered him a salary of five dollars a week to tour the nearest counties with him. A.P. went home that night with a decision to make. By the time he reached the Carter cabin he had made up his mind. He would take the chance and travel with the "physick" show.

He awoke at dawn and met the wagon just as it was pulling out of town. He had not told his parents of his plans but left a note behind telling them where he would be. A.P. knew they would have opposed his decision. The "physick" wagon creaked north to Dickinson County. It was as though A.P. Carter was searching for an answer without being aware of the search. They stopped at the county seat shortly after dusk and set up shop across from a church. That night, even in the darkness, A.P. could see the cross next to the church's whitewashed door.

The next morning the medicine man shook A.P. out of bed at dawn; he told the young man it was part of his job to set up the wagon before every show. This was an unpleasant surprise! A.P. protested, and the medicine man offered him an extra dollar a show if he would help set it up.

Later A.P. sang on the rear of the wagon. The crowd was large, and the medicine man did a good business. After the show A.P. retired to a local tavern to sing and drink. He stayed late and awoke the next morning with a fuzzy head. The wagon had to be packed up and moved out of town and A.P. barely got the job done. He had never taken a drink until he began selling fruit trees, and then he had not drunk every day. Now, with

A.P.'s singing becoming popular all over their route, drinking became a daily affair. Every morning the headaches and listlessness got worse.

On the morning they came into Maces Spring, he could hardly be forced out of bed by the medicine man. The crowd gathered by late morning, knowing that a "physick" show with A. P. Carter would be there. His performances that day were disastrous. With his body and mind weakened by the unaccustomed drinking, A.P.'s singing lacked its usual power and depth. The crowd, composed of his friends and neighbors, thinned out in embarrassment. Very little patent medicine was sold that day.

That night A.P. headed toward a tavern with his friends. His minister recognized him and stopped to talk. He convinced the young man not to drink that night. Instead, A.P. went with the minister to his home and talked until early in the morning. The minister read to him from the Bible and talked of the damage a man can do to himself with alcohol. The minister did not hector him, however, and A.P. began to understand where his drinking habit could lead him.

The next morning he quit the "physick" show and went back to selling fruit trees. He had learned a lesson some other country-music artists were never to understand. This young man from the mountains had an early exposure to the pressures and temptations of the business. The constant traveling, the lack of roots, the easy temptation to believe those who would overpraise you—all of this convinced A.P. to avoid this path when he later became a professional musician. His experience as a young man made him a wiser performer when success unexpectedly burst upon him.

A. P. Carter's sin may seem minor to people of our day. Most of us have heard similar austere chronicles, stories of a rural Christian's acceptance of God's Will. The sin seems nothing more than a certain bored restlessness which leads a young man or woman into drinking. But beneath this description is a truth which goes to the heart of southern rural consciousness—sin is a part of the human condition. A.P. had been reared in an environment which took Christian values for granted. Life was hard—it was a struggle to survive. But the Christian virtues were won by fierce struggle. It is sometimes necessary to break rules in order to learn their value. Paradoxes of this sort make for better Christians.

The minister led him back on God's path because Alvin Pleasant had seen that the way of the Lord was the only way. It is only when one sees the options clearly laid out that it is possible to embrace the Lord with certaintly. One has seen the dreadful consequences of the other path.

He went home to the Carter cabin and persevered in the sale of fruit trees. His sales were better until the fall planting season ended. He was then forced to look for work elsewhere. Luckily, during his sales trips he had met a blacksmith in Gate City. The man offered him a job helping around his shop during the winter months, and A.P. gratefully accepted.

It was during this job that A.P. received the nickname Doc. During the winter the horseshoe business generally fell off, and the work in the shop consisted of repairing and maintaining farm machinery. It was the first time A.P. had done any serious work with tools, and he took to it immediately. Since his family had never owned many farm implements of the advanced sort, he, perhaps, found their intricacy fascinating. A.P.'s mechanical ability amazed the blacksmith. When patrons arrived with a piece of malfunctioning machinery, the blacksmith told them to "see the doctor," pointing toward the rear of the barn where A.P. worked. The name stuck.

The winter passed quickly, and Doc earned more money than he ever had before. As spring came to the mountains, the horseshoe business picked up again. The blacksmith hired more help and kept Doc in the back room with the machinery. But the repair work slacked off, and Doc was back on the road selling fruit trees one or two days a week.

It was 1914. On the other side of the Atlantic the nations of Europe were preparing for war. But you could not sense the world's turmoil in the peaceful stillness of Scott County.

Doc rode an old quarter horse over the trail leading

to the other side of Clinch Mountain. He rode into the neighborhood of Copper Creek, Old Muddy Mossican, and Addington Frame. He traveled past small, rapid streams, rolling hills, big two-story houses, wooden rail fences, and cellars packed with potatoes and cabbage. Doc enjoyed visiting in this part of the county. He knew many people here: the Kilgores, Mill Nicholas over in Addington Frame, the McConnells, and the Addingtons. He intended to drop in on the McConnells first; but they were in the fields, so he rode over in the direction of his Aunt Susie's cabin.

She had never had more money than her neighbors, but her homestead was larger than most. It was a full five minutes after Doc rode through the gate that the sound of the singing reached him. The wind was gusting. The melody, carried along on the air, came to him in bits and snatches. The wind grew still, and he heard the entire song wafting over toward him. It was a girl's voice, very high, and its pure tone pierced his heart. But then the wind picked up again, and the melody's structure seemed to shatter. Doc was only then aware of a voice singing low up ahead.

He rode on until he came to the cabin. The singing stopped. Aunt Susie, his mother's aunt by marriage to Doc Nickles, Mollie's maternal uncle, stepped out on the porch and waved him inside the house. Sales were always best made in long conversation, and there would probably be one that day. Doc had not seen his

Aunt Susie in quite a long time. Doc dismounted and walked inside the house. He hugged his Aunt Susie, and she offered him a cup of tea.

Suddenly, the singing began again. It seemed to come from the front room. It was the same voice. "Who's singing?" Doc asked. Aunt Susie pointed to a doorway. They walked over and peered through. Inside, a young woman, in a pale yellow dress, sat with an Autoharp on her lap. Her face was averted and she did not notice them. She tapped her feet in time with the chords as she sang the plaintive song "Engine 143." It was the tale of an engineer who ran fast to make up lost time, and thus died for the engine he loved.

Aunt Susie smiled and took Doc's hand. Together they walked slowly and quietly into the parlor where the girl sang. She did not notice when he went over and stood behind her. He began to sing bass as she came to the last few lyrics. Surprised, she turned to glance up at him, but her singing did not falter. Doc did not know why he had not recognized her before. It was Sara Dougherty, the girl who had been raised by his Uncle Milburn since her parents died.

The fruit trees were forgotten. Aunt Susie tactfully withdrew from the room. As the two of them talked, Doc noticed the strange, shy lilt in her voice, and the warm glow in her eyes. Her parents had died when she was a very young child. The ten children of Elizabeth and Sevier Dougherty were scattered among the kinfolk, as almost always happened in the mountains when children were orphaned. She now lived with Uncle Mill Nicholas and his wife and was on a visit with her Aunt Susie.

She wore her hair short, and it was closely cropped all around her head. Her high forehead was an excellent preparation for the black, penetrating eyes. Her mouth had to be coaxed into smiling, but when she did condescend, her face became radiant. When she stood to escort him out to the porch, she was almost as tall as he was. He had never known a tall, buxom, young woman like Sara Dougherty.

Her voice was the most remarkable thing about her. It was very low for a woman, and if Doc had known the word "contralto" he would have used it. But her voice was more than that. It wavered just a trifle as she sang, and the sincerity of her singing sent tingles up his spine. It was a voice he could listen to forever. He enjoyed singing bass with her—he liked it better than singing in a tavern. His voice tucked itself neatly within hers. In the tavern, the men's voices often cracked as they tried to reach for notes which were beyond them. And no man Doc had ever heard had this measure of sincere feeling in his voice. He rebuked himself, wondering how he could have overlooked this girl in the past.

They talked until an orange band appeared along the horizon. Doc discovered that she knew more songs than he did. He listened in amazement as she reeled off song titles as quickly as she could—half of them had names he did not recognize. He gained permission to see her again at the Nicholas homestead when she went home from her visit.

He left Aunt Susie's house with his fruit trees unsold.

# 5

# Coming Together

*Having then gifts differing according to the grace that is given to us. . . .*

Romans 12:6

For a year Sara and Doc exchanged visits and correspondence. In the mountains courtship is a rigid ritual. The initial meeting had to be followed by a period of waiting; during this time Sara and Doc got to know each other through letters and formal visits. Finally Doc asked Mill Nicholas for Sara's hand, and they were married on June 18, 1915, at the Nicholas homestead in Copper Creek, Scott County.

Doc Carter knew he had married quite a musician. Sara Dougherty had been exposed to music since childhood. Her first real teacher was a neighbor, Eb Easterland, who played the Autoharp and knew many old songs. The Autoharp is one of America's representative folk instruments, and Easterland played it as well as anybody in Scott County. Sara never became a true virtuoso on this instrument. In later years, during performances of the Carter Family she never played the melody on the instrument—she preferred to play chords to provide the rhythm for other instruments.

Mill Nicholas was a fiddler. On weekends Sara would join him and his friend Ap Harris, a neighborhood fiddler who lived a few miles away. Crowds would gather on these occasions and Sara had her first taste of performing before an audience. When Doc was seeing Sara regularly he would sometimes join the performers.

After their marriage, Doc built a cabin for Sara and himself on land given him by his father. His relatives and friends participated in a cabin raising to help him. His sales job with the nursery became more profitable, as if the matrimonial state provided an increase in his powers of salesmanship. Sara cultivated a large garden and raised several goats. Quitting his job at the blacksmith shop, Doc occasionally took in work and did repairs in the small barn he built on the land. He also began a carpentry business and occasionally made furniture for his neighbors in the valley.

If anything, their musical involvement increased

after the marriage. The society of Scott County had always been close-knit, and visits between relatives and friends were frequent. At least once a week people stopped around, or the newlyweds visited others. Invariably they would be asked to sing, and instruments would be produced. Doc played the fiddle and the old songs were sung again. They acted exactly as they had all during their lives. Music just naturally assumed an important role in their lives.

They sang every week for their neighbors, and their musical skills improved greatly as time passed. Other good musicians from all over the valley joined them from week to week. Postman Price Owens played fiddle; the three of them enjoyed making music together and formed a group for a short time.

Music and religion were equally important in their lives. They sang all the hymns. Spiritual music was the material they loved the most. Doc often visited churches during his sales trips. He would always try to see the minister or church organist and ask them for songs he did not know. In this way, almost without realizing it, Doc Carter was serving as a living repository of sacred mountain music, preserving it for future generations.

The young Carters became adept at church music during their first year of marriage and were so popular that they were invited to sing at the Newhope Methodist Church at Christmastime. It was in this way that Doc Carter continued his musical career. Offerings were almost certainly taken at this performance, as they were at subsequent musical appearances. But through the early years of their marriage these performances did in no sense constitute a true professional career—although the thought of this possibility never left Doc's mind. Although Doc and Sara sang almost anywhere they were asked to perform, and were often paid for these performances, they did not make much money from music in the years before 1927. Their livelihood was their land. Whatever could be wrested from it was theirs, along with the money Doc made from his handiwork. This state of affairs was changed by their association with Maybelle Addington.

Sara's kinfolk were in Copper Creek, and the relatives visited back and forth quite often. Maybelle Addington, born on May 10, 1909, was only six years old at the time of Sara and Doc's marriage. When they would play music on Uncle Mill's front porch, little Maybelle would often visit them. She was Sara's first cousin. They especially enjoyed the youngster because, of all the Addingtons and other folk who came to watch them, little Maybelle was the best dancer to the music. She would sway back and forth, dancing all over the porch, while Sara and Doc picked and sang. Even at that young age, Maybelle tried to get into the act on occasion, speaking up in the middle of one of cousin Sara's renditions and asking if she could sing along too.

As Maybelle grew older she became proficient on

the banjo, Autoharp, and the guitar. Although her family was quite religious, as were most people in Scott County, there was no outright prohibition against stringed instruments. Maybelle received early encouragement from her mother, who was the leader of the women's chorus in the Fair Oak Methodist Church. Unlike Sara and Doc, Maybelle's forte was not vocal. Instruments were her real love, and she cultivated that love with an obsessive passion. She began on the Autoharp, learning the conventional methods of play. The "harp" is a board on which piano-like strings are stretched. The harpist presses keys, which are suspended above the strings, and in this way produces chords. It is an excellent instrument for the rural musician. One is able to carry it along almost anywhere, and it provides a clear, and relatively easy background to any song in the rural repertoire.

Before Maybelle Carter, however, no one had thought of going beyond these conventional methods. At the age of twelve she began to pick out melodies on the Autoharp. At that time it was a revolutionary achievement. It was for this reason, alone, that Maybelle became known throughout Scott County. The music-conscious hill people realized that Maybelle was a prodigy. For most people, moreover, this new way of playing the Autoharp would have been accomplishment enough. But it was not enough for Maybelle.

She next turned to the banjo, learning to play it as well as anyone in the county. Up to this time it was unusual for a woman to learn the banjo at all—let alone learn it as well as, or better than, a man. Maybelle's intense love for music gave her the determination to break the sexual barrier.

All of this would have gone unrecorded, however, if Maybelle had not finally decided to learn the guitar, the instrument which would make her famous. She first learned the conventional chords and methods of picking out a melody from Eb Easterland, Sara's teacher. When she perfected this Maybelle went far beyond him. She learned to pick the melody out on the three bass strings, while simultaneously strumming the rhythm out on the top three treble strings (which are normally reserved for the melody).

Maybelle thus pioneered a style which was to be copied by countless country-music musicians who would come after her. The method she used has come to be called the thumb-pluck 'n' fingers-brush right-hand pattern by folk-music enthusiasts. Basically, this describes a method of play in which the thumb picks out the melody on the low strings, while the other fingers strum out the rhythm. At first Maybelle used no picks at all. She later claimed she did not know they existed, but that is probably an ironic exaggeration. When her professional career began in earnest,

Maybelle used picks for the first time, but her unique brand of guitar work remained as excellent as it had always been.

From her earliest days Maybelle Addington played with Sara. They were raised up together, as Virgie Carter Hobbs has testified. There was only a quarter of a mile distance between Maybelle's home and Sara's place. They were together so often that they soon took each other for granted, and Sara took on the role of big sister. But the difference in their ages pulled them apart when Sara reached fifteen and began to think of marriage. They saw each other less frequently. However, after the marriage Maybelle continued to visit Maces Spring from Copper Creek and a deeper, more adult friendship grew up between them. Doc joined their music-making, and they conducted quite an intense musical education among themselves.

It was about this time that Doc began to go on song-collecting trips around the neighboring counties. It was during these early trips that he gathered material for the group's repertoire from the people he would meet on his travels. After he gathered these songs he would "do them up in our style." In those times he was filling the role of the folklorist who deliberately sets out to collect and record the indigenous music of an area. Doc did not think of himself as a folklorist, for he was simply a man who liked to sing and who was constantly on the lookout for songs that sang well. This love affair with the music of his people has preserved their legacy for us.

In 1922 Maybelle's family moved to Bristol. She was now closer to Maces Spring, and the musical interchange with Sara and Doc became an almost daily occurrence. It did not matter whether there was an audience or not. On many a warm night during the summer Maybelle, who had arrived at dusk, would be sitting on the front steps plucking her guitar. Sara would sit on the porch swing, strumming the rhythms on her Autoharp and singing the song in a clear voice. Doc would stand directly behind her and sing bass when the song began. But, as the song went on, he would stroll around the porch while he sang. The three of them were, by this time, accomplished mountain musicians. They had all the skills they would need for an artistically successful musical career.

Meanwhile Maybelle was growing up in other ways. She began seeing Doc's younger brother, Ezra Carter, on a more serious basis—before E.J. had just been around, like any other Carter brother or sister. They began to court in the late summer of 1925 exchanging letters and visits much as Sara and Doc had done. They were married on March 13, 1926, in Bristol, where E.J. had gotten himself a job with the railroad.

As in the case of Sara and Doc, Maybelle's musical activity was accelerated by her marriage. She traveled around Scott County, playing her banjo or guitar at barn dances for the sheer fun of it, and she made herself well known in the area. When there were no dances to play, and Doc and Sara were unavailable, Maybelle would stay up all night long with her brothers, strumming the banjo and listening to all the songs they knew.

Lest it sound as though Sara, Maybelle, and Doc were living amidst a literal "land of milk and honey," it has to be said that it was sometimes difficult for them to "look on the sunny side." The thirties brought Depression for urban America. In the twenties the Depression in rural America was just as real, and just as hard. Doc's sales job at the nursery ended in the mid-twenties. The trees he had sold before were just as fertile, but there was no market for them. He managed to keep active his association with the blacksmith in Gate City; but there were fewer calls for horseshoes and when farm machinery broke down, it stayed that way. There was no money to fix it.

The Carter homestead expanded, hard times or no. Two years after their wedding Sara had given birth to Gladys. By the mid-twenties there were two more children, Jeanette and Joe. There was a greater need for money, and Doc never stopped looking for ways to bring it into the house.

Perhaps this is one explanation for Doc's increasing interest in a musical career. Unlike even the most accomplished musicians in the mountains, A. P. Carter knew that money could be made in the music business. From the beginning of their marriage Doc pressed Sara into performances, even though she really preferred to sing only for herself or a few friends. He was a tireless promoter, although Doc himself had never heard the word. He rode about on his song-collecting trips with a dual purpose. Collecting the music was his first goal, but he would especially look for opportunities to perform. Visiting ministers was a good way to book performances. This was his favorite method, mainly because he enjoyed singing spiritual music in a church atmosphere. If a church was not available, the people were asked whether they would come and pay to hear the Carters sing. By this time the Carters were well-known throughout the area, and the answer to Doc's question was usually yes.

Doc believed in the music the Carter Family was making, but his vision of a professional career was not shared by Sara. Sara thought that singing spiritual music for money was not right—she said so in no uncertain terms. Doc disagreed, saying, if people were willing to pay to hear their music, there was nothing sinful about it. Besides, he would add, we need extra money, and there's no harm in making it this way.

Maybelle also had her doubts. She was (and to some extent still is) a fundamentally private person, and she was nervous about singing before audiences. However, she had no scruples about making a bit of money in the process. Doc arranged more appearances than she would have liked, and he set up some dates without first asking her. Several times she had to refuse because she did not want to become a complete stranger to her new husband. E. J. Carter played the fiddle himself and he encouraged his wife's musical talent. Maybelle simply did not want to give him a reason to go against her music. E.J. and Maybelle had to struggle to keep their heads above water, as did everybody else in Scott County. A musical career was a luxury to the Carters, an avocation which Maybelle thought impossible to convert into a vocation.

Doc Carter was becoming eccentric—he was entertaining an idea which was pure fantasy in his environment! By the mid-twenties he had come to realize that people would be willing to pay to hear the three of them sing. The lack of money undoubtedly made him look in this direction; but there were many musicians in Scott County, and little money, and A. P. Carter was the only one to actively think "career." He began to take even more unusual risks in the furtherance of a career.

In the late summer of 1925 Doc rode home in excitement. He had been touring the farms around Bristol in an effort to sell fruit trees, but a conversation with a man in Bristol had made him abruptly turn around for home.

Whenever he was in Bristol Doc would stop at Cecil

McClister's record store. Cy had often been of help to Doc; he knew almost every good musician for a hundred miles around, and had told Doc of many people who gave him new songs. For the past year Cy had been playing a few country-music records which had come into his store. As Doc listened to them he wondered how the musicians had convinced the record company to record them. Cy could not tell him, but the record store proprietor kept Doc's question in mind.

On this day in late summer Cecil McClister had exciting news for Doc. A representative from the Brunswick Record Company had stopped at the store and asked if any good hillbilly musicians lived around Bristol. Doc and Cy laughed about it. Cy told him the man wanted to see Doc, Sara, and Maybelle. He wanted to put some musicians on record, and he would pay up to twenty-five dollars.

Doc could not believe it! The record company was willing to put him on record, and to pay him for it in the process! Of course he would do it, he told Cy. The man from the record company was staying in a hotel in Bristol, but did not have a phone in his room. If Doc could come back in an hour, Cy would try to arrange a day when Doc could meet with the record company man.

Doc went out to lunch but he was barely able to eat. The act of making a record was a complete mystery to him and he spent most of the hour wondering what it was like. He knew the words: microphone, recording horn, and transcription disk. Cecil McClister used these terms when he talked about records, but he only sold records, and had never seen one made. Cy could not even produce photos of these things. Doc was left to imagine how they would look. Soon it was time to return to the record store and Cy gave him a date. He would meet the man from Brunswick in an old storefront on the outskirts of the city. The man wanted to see the three of them, since Cy had spoken highly of all the Carters.

Doc rode up to his cabin, and met Sara pulling weeds in the garden. She looked surprised when she saw him, since he rarely interrupted his sales trips in the middle of the day to come home. "A man from the Brunswick Record Company wants to make a record of our singing," he told her. "And he'll pay us twenty-five dollars." As she was later to tell it, Sara did not really want to make a record. They had been performing quite a bit in the area recently, and she was tired. Besides, the house needed work, and chores had piled up. Things needed doing, and Sara did not believe a trip to Bristol would help her do them any faster.

But there was always the problem of money, and Doc's mention of the twenty-five dollars forced Sara to reconsider. The sum was by far more than they had ever been paid for a single performance. Taxes were coming due again, and the children needed new shoes. Sara could not refuse to go with Doc, but she made him promise to slow down for a while and give her a rest after the record was made.

Maybelle was another matter. E.J. had been called out of town recently by the railroad, and she and the children had been allowed to come along. The family would be living down in Roanoke for more than a month. Maybelle was simply unavailable for the session.

On a morning in early September, Doc and Sara used a borrowed wagon to travel down the narrow paths to Kingsport, Tennessee. This was a small community on the outskirts of Bristol in which the record company man had rented the storefront. Roads were being built all through the area with the increasing popularity of the automobile, but there was, as yet, no road from Maces Spring in the direction of Bristol. Their wagon broke down when they were halfway there, and the journey took them four hours.

They pulled into Kingsport and found the address just after noon. Doc worried all through the trip that they were too late, but the man from Brunswick, whose name Doc was later to forget, told them they were just on time. He asked them to wait in the front of the store with the other musicians while he recorded them, one at a time, in the back room.

This was one of the very earliest rural recording

sessions; as such, it has great interest for the country-music fan. Unfortunately, no historical record survives of this session. We only know of it today through A.P. Carter's hazy recollection. However, although Doc did not recall names and dates, his memory for some aspects of the experience was sharp.

Doc had never seen so many banjo-pickers, fiddlers, singers, guitar-pickers, and other musicians in one place before. There were at least twenty groups crowded into the brightly lit front room. One wall was completely covered by display windows, and it was a hot and sunny day. At one o'clock the sun poured directly through the windows, casting shadows of the expectant musicians up against the unwashed wall of the room. There was a buzz of conversation in the room for a while, then they all fell silent occasionally and listened. But no sounds could be heard coming from the back room. Some wag wondered if the record man had descended with the musicians into the cellar. Otherwise it was difficult to understand how a raucous band could not be heard through the thin walls of the back room.

The musicians all talked in surprised, half-amused voices, as if they could not understand why they had taken the time to be there—crowded into an extremely hot room of an abandoned storefront. The conversation stopped abruptly when a man in a black-striped suit appeared at the door to the back room and motioned to

Doc and Sara. They were escorted into a dark, musty, curtain-draped room.

Both Doc and Sara could barely see. "Watch your step!" someone called, and the man took Doc's elbow and led the couple to the microphone. It was a silvery plate on the end of a black horn which protruded from a mass of curtains. Doc's eyes gradually adjusted to the light; he saw music stands stacked in a corner, and a black man, sitting at an upright piano, grinning over at him.

"Are you comfortable? Did you bring all your instruments? Is that one all you have?" The man indicated Sara's Autoharp which she was cradling across her lap. Doc nodded yes. The man introduced himself, with a name Doc did not remember, and began to talk about the operation of the temporary recording studio. The windows and the walls were hung with heavy curtains he explained, because the recording machine was very sensitive to echoes, and the curtains helped to deaden them. One was to sing very loudly and as clearly as one could, while playing the accompaniment softly.

The man placed them around the microphone and instructed them to keep their faces close to the metallic surface. They were to project their voices in its direction. When Doc and Sara promised to do this, he asked them what songs they had brought. Could he see the sheet music? They laughed and explained that all their music was in their heads. The record company man looked disconcerted—after a moment, he joined in their laughter. He was new to this area, he told them, and had never before heard country music. He was not used to recording performers without sheet music, but since it seemed no one in the area used written notes, he would have to do without it. He would rely only on the sound of the record when they finished singing, he told them.

Taking out a pad and a pen he asked Doc what songs he planned to sing. Thirty years after the event, A. P. Carter could only recall one of the songs they sang on that hot afternoon. Thus we know only that "Anchored in Love" was a song recorded on that day. This song was later to become a Carter Family classic. Doc claimed that they sang it as well as they could that day. The song spoke of life's dangers and the rewards after death.

They began to sing. The record man kept motioning to Sara to keep her Autoharp's tone down, but she paid him no mind. She could not play it any more softly. Sara began in that piercingly sincere voice, and A.P. backed her up with his quavering bass, a voice that most people said "had a tear in it." When they got to the chorus he sang the lyrics slightly after Sara did. This practice was imported, along with the song, from Elizabethan England, where the singing styles of the mountains had their roots.

Without Maybelle's guitar, their rendition sounded

somewhat flat to Doc. When they finished singing, the record company man asked if they wanted to sing it a second time, to see if it could be done better. Doc and Sara readily agreed, and the black pianist agreed to back them up, in an attempt to make up for the absence of Maybelle's melodic lead. The second time around, their voices had greater intensity when they came to the final chorus and reaffirmed their faith in that anchor—love Divine.

The sentiments of the song were feelings nurtured over a lifetime of living in the mountains. They sang of death, but there was no despair in their voices, or in the words. The world beyond this earth often seemed more real to the country dweller of Doc and Sara's time. Death was a fact of life for these people. (The availability of medical care in the mountains was meager, if it existed at all.) Unlike the people of contemporary America, the mountain folk could not hide from the realities of life by immersing themselves in an artificial world created by Madison Avenue. Death was a part of life to be faced squarely. It was not shunted out of mind by euphemism and misdirection. Death was not a "passing away"—not the "last sleep." Trees, deer, dogs, and man died, but the human race had an understanding of God, and that was the difference. One did not sleep at the time of death, one awakened to a greater life.

"The danger is past" when one has passed life's test.

During one's time on earth, there are no certainties. A man is weak. He may often act contrary to his own best interests, and the divine injunctions of the Lord. The acceptance of the Lord brings certainty. One is "anchored in love divine," and granted eternal life by a compassionate Creator.

They finished the second version of the song. The record company man appeared at their side, thanked them for coming, and handed them twenty-five dollars in cash. Sara had never before seen so much money in one lump sum. (In those hard times twenty-five dollars was almost equal to two months of income.) Sara later recalled that it felt somehow dishonest to take the money. "It wasn't work for me to sing, I wouldn't have gotten so much money if I had done a wash for the entire county."

The man from Brunswick promised he would contact them if their song had been made into a record, but he did not offer them a contract. Doc Carter was confused about the record business at the time. "I guess I didn't know anything about the music business then," he later recalled. "I thought it was automatic; the records would just be in the store a few weeks after we sang into the microphone. It didn't seem that they would go to all that trouble for nothing."

But that was exactly the case. Brunswick was roaming the southern mountains with little idea of what it wanted. It knew even less about what would sell. Still thinking in terms of an urban buying public, the company men and field recording agents used their urban tastes to judge the music they recorded. Doc and Sara did not fit into their marketing plans.

They left Bristol, riding the wagon back home along the narrow path. When they resumed their routine, the recording session was soon forgotten. Luckily times began to improve somewhat. Doc regained his job at the nursery when the owner asked him to do some handiwork around the grounds. His sales picked up when a bit more money began to flow through Scott County. It was the "trickle down" system. Urban America was roaring along in the wake of a bull market, and some of the money was finding its way into the backlands.

As A. P. Carter later said, "I thought at the time it was the twenty-five dollars that turned us around." Whatever caused the turn of good fortune, times were better than they had been for the Carters in a long while, perhaps better than they had ever been. Doc strengthened his ties with the Friendly Grove Methodist Church and began to lead a chorus there. He trained many local children in the ways of mountain music. Sara and Maybelle sang in the chorus too, and Doc continued to collect songs on his sales trips. Much to Sara's delight his thoughts of a musical career seemed to be fading in the background.

Doc Carter kept up his friendship with Cecil McClister. Even though he did not own a phonograph or buy records, when passing through Bristol on sales trips he would stop to rest the horses and chat with Cy. The record-store owner fancied himself a music-business insider, and in a sense he was right. In that place and time he was the closest thing to it. Doc, Sara, Maybelle, and some of their friends were now playing before audiences about once a month. Cy directed Doc to some of these engagements and people were constantly coming to his shop and asking for the Carter Family. Cy had to turn away almost everybody, on Doc's orders, and he had an idea of the Carters' commercial potential.

On a summer day in 1927, a northerner came around to the shop and asked for local talent. Cy told him about many people, including the Carters, and he informed Doc about the visitor. Doc said he was easing off as far as singing was concerned, but Cy refused to believe him. He said Doc's family had a talent, and the world would find its way to them sooner or later. The world was opening up, Cy believed—things weren't going to be the same anymore.

Doc brought up the Brunswick session, but the record-store owner waved this objection away. "Most of these city fellows from the record companies don't know what to listen for," he explained. There were no experts in this field. "But this fellow who came in yesterday seems to know what he is doing. He says he works for Victor," Cy added.

Doc Carter later remembered his reaction to this

news. He did not want to get his hopes up again. There was probably no way to make real money in this music business, for the musician at least. But Cy urged him on, and his natural desire came back. Victor was the best-known record company in America. If they had somebody who knew what he was talking about, the Carter Family might have a chance.

Cy promised to tell him if the Victor man returned, and Doc said he would be back in Bristol in a day or two. He then rode home, dreading the talk he would have with Sara. If she refused to go to Bristol again, he would not record alone. Their life was coming together, and if Sara objected to recording (and he went despite this) there would be conflict. He had a responsibility to avoid that.

Surprisingly, Sara was agreeable. She asked if they would be paid for it, and Doc had to admit that he did not know. She smiled and touched his cheek. Doc remembers her saying, "You really want to make a record, Doc?" He nodded, and she laughed. "As it says in Romans," she said, 'Having then gifts differing according to the grace given to us . . . .' Your gifts, Doc, lead you on!" (*See* Romans 12:6.) Doc protested. Maybelle and Sara had the bulk of the talent, he told her. He just wanted to let people know about it. They teased back and forth for the better part of an hour. He said he would quit his job and start a musical career after the audition, and they laughed.

Doc then went riding over to Maybelle and E.J.'s

cabin. Maybelle and her husband agreed that the record should be made, if the company asked. Maybelle was quite eager to come along and at first did not realize that she was to record also. "Should I bring my guitar, Doc?" she asked, and he and his younger brother laughed. "If you don't, I don't think it's worth doing," Doc finally replied.

Two days later Doc returned to Bristol. Cecil McClister told him the man from Victor whose name was Ralph Peer, was anxious to hear them. He would have room for them on August 1, 1927.

# 6

# The Recording Machine

*The songs . . . reflected the truth of their environment, told of its poverty, hardship, loneliness . . . . their art served to transcend these sorrows . . . .*

Maybelle Carter crossed the mountains between Poor Valley and Maces Spring in the late afternoon of July 31, 1927. She and E.J. had recently moved back into the mountains, as they had missed the quiet of those peaks. E.J. had been transferred by the railroad and was now forced to travel throughout the state of Virginia for weeks at a time. He was the foreman of a track repair crew, and there was simply not enough work for him around Bristol.

Maybelle was often lonely for Eck (as she had begun

to call him), especially now, when she was six months pregnant. She was able to spend more time with Sara and Doc, however. They were now honing their music, and she felt comfortable singing with them. Doc knew more songs than anyone else she knew, and every time she visited them there was always a new song to learn. Maybelle spent the night before the recording session in their cabin. They would have to get up early to make it to Bristol on time, and Doc and Sara would need help with their kids, since they were taking them all along.

In the morning they all rose early. Doc, as usual, was the hardest to arouse, and he snored until the aroma of morning coffee wafted his way and woke him up. Sara and Maybelle prepared a big country breakfast and packed sandwiches they had made the night before. After the dishes were cleared away, they all piled into an old Model T which Doc had borrowed from his boss at the nursery.

It was twenty-five miles to Bristol, Tennessee. They drove on a new road which passed through Maces Spring on its way to Bristol. It was still, however, more suited to horse-drawn wagons than automobiles. There were six people in the jalopy: Doc, Sara, Maybelle, and Doc and Sara's children, Gladys, Jeanette, and baby Joe. The road was not paved; at some points motorists were forced to ford streams, since there were few bridges along the route. It was in such a place that Doc's car broke down. Everyone had to get out and push the jalopy through a stream to the other side. The

Model T had to sit for a half-hour until the ignition dried out. It was late in the morning. They brought out the sandwiches and sat on the sideboard. Having no watch, Doc fretted that they would be late. Sara tried to reassure him. Besides, the record company man would certainly wait for them if they were not on time. Did he remember the first recording session? The car was started soon afterwards, and the rest of the journey to Bristol was uneventful. It was their entrance into the city which was strangely exciting.

They drove down Bristol's main street, which was the dividing line between the states of Tennessee and Virginia. Traffic was unusually heavy, and during the long stops Maybelle explained to the children that one side of the street was in Virginia and the other was in Tennessee. Gladys wanted to get out of the car and stand with one foot in Virginia, and the other in Tennessee, but Doc told her to stay in the car.

As they drove into the heart of the business district they began to see people carrying musical instruments—banjos, Autoharps, bass fiddles, and guitars. They saw some people they knew—musicians with whom they had played. "What's going on?" Maybelle remembers Doc shouted down to one of them, "Is there a fiddler's convention?" The man, who was a fiddler, shouted back that they were all in town to make records, that a man was here who was willing to record anyone, and that they had all come to stay in town until he would give them a chance.

Sara grimaced. She asked Doc if it was going to be like the last time. Would they have to wait in small rooms with scores of other musicians? Doc assured her that Mr. Peer, the man from Victor, had said that this time was just for them. (He had heard that Peer was recording everybody in sight. But Doc did not mind that. There were many fine fiddlers, pickers, and singers in the hills. Why not give everybody a crack at making a record?)

There was a frail young man in Bristol on that day, a man the Carters had never met, but with whom they were to share a rich, although brief, professional relationship. His name was Jimmie Rodgers, and he had a date to record with Mr. Peer and Victor, just as the Carters did. It is one of the mythic coincidences of country-music history. During one brief period of time, in one place, under the direction of one man, the two greatest country artists of the twenties and thirties were to have their starts.

After a long search Doc found a safe parking place for the Model T. He tied it up to a hitching post (as motorists still did in the backcountry when the hand brake failed and was not repaired). The Carters walked down the wood-planked sidewalks toward the location of the recording session, a room above Cecil McClister's record store. Miraculously they were not late but they could not stop to rest if they were to arrive on time.

Ralph Peer was standing under the awning of the record store when they arrived. The Carters must have been quite oblivious to their appearance. Doc wore a pair of full overalls, and there were dried splotches of mud up and down the garment. Sara and Maybelle both wore calico dresses, and the children were poorly dressed. They were backwoods people, and they were not accustomed to being in town. It was a confrontation of the rural tradition with northern commercial music. We do not know what Doc, Sara, or Maybelle thought of Ralph Peer's appearance. It would be safe to say, however, that they had never met anyone like him.

According to Maybelle, not all of the children followed them into the dark, cool, satin-curtained room. Although they wanted to see this mysterious thing called "making a record," it was simply impossible. The recording engineer was nervous—he was not used to an invasion of a backwoods family into the hushed sanctuary of his studio. In New York such things were unimaginable.

Mr. Peer convinced the Carters to leave the youngest child outside, as a compromise. Maybelle Carter remembers Gladys being saddled with the baby-sitting chore, since she was the oldest child. (She was then nine years old, and Joe was just big enough to walk about by holding onto Gladys' hand.) At first they walked up and down the hall outside the temporary recording studio, but Joe began to cry, and Gladys had to take him downstairs. They strolled the street in the bright sunlight; Joe's sobs ceased only when his sister bought him an ice cream cone.

Inside the hotel room, the Carters noticed how different this room was from the Brunswick studio, which Sara and Doc had previously described to Maybelle. Despite the unnatural darkness and heavy curtains, there was an air of relaxed friendliness in the room. Ralph Peer did his best to make them at home, asking first about their hometown, and making other conversation designed to put them at ease.

The recording instruments were different too. Gone was the mysterious horn, and the bright metal plate. There was no longer a need to shove one's face into the plate—to sing loudly and unnaturally. There was now an instrument, made of bright chrome, which was in the shape of a round tobacco tin. It was fixed on top of a metal pole attached to a base on the floor. A wire ran down to the floor from the upright object; it continued along the baseboards and went out under a door leading to another room.

It was "electrical recording," Ralph Peer explained. The old horns were gone because they did not give a good quality to the sound. The tobacco tin was called a "microphone." Because of it, they would not have to stand close. They could arrange themselves in perfectly natural positions. The important fact that they were to remember in later years was that they could sing naturally, as they did at home.

Mr. Peer was not an ordinary talent scout from the city. Unlike the man from Brunswick, Ralph Peer knew exactly what he wanted. He now looked for one element in his auditions of country artists. Was there a quality about them, something the rural record-buyers could immediately identify? If he found this quality, he would record the country artists again, delving into their repertoire until he found material which emphasized this one quality. Peer would be called an experienced producer today. He knew intuitively how singers would sound on record, whether their voices could be produced adequately by the primitive recording technology of his time.

Peer questioned them about their musical background. He was soon amazed at these people who had chanced into his studio. Their repertoire was extensive, as varied as some highly successful northern artists Peer knew. They had ample performing experience which gave them a calm self-assurance. And, they had recorded before. Peer had never seen such a contrast between behavior and appearance.

Although dressed in dirty overalls and faded calico dresses, these mountain people behaved as professionals, ready to do their best on cue. If their talent was as polished as their manner, Ralph Peer must have thought, I have quite a find.

The blank disk was cued in; Mr. Peer told them to begin singing when he raised his hand. Doc remained standing, as he always did, and Sara and Maybelle sat before the microphone. Sara cradled her Autoharp, and Maybelle held her guitar (a Gibson she had bought during the last year). She would provide the musical introduction to the song.

Peer raised his hand, and the Carter Family sang "Weeping Willow." The lyrics were based on Psalms 137:2. Maybelle completed the instrumental introduction, and Sara and Doc began to sing, their voices harmonizing perfectly. "We hanged our harps upon the willows. . . ." Sara sang in a clear voice, with Doc's bass harmonizing behind her. Peer's reaction was immediate. "As soon as I heard Sara's voice, that was it!" he later said. He had trained himself to watch for one element which could highlight a record. Sara's voice fitted perfectly into his pattern. When the song was finished Peer rushed back into the recording room and played back the test disk. He could not believe his luck. Peer had not expected to find anything this exciting in Bristol.

Peer's engineer commented that they took well and the Victor talent scout nodded his agreement. Sara's voice was perfect for recording, and the group's level of performance and harmonizing was high. Peer played the record over several times and invited the three Carters into the back room to hear themselves on record.

Their reactions are not known, but Mr. Peer was enthusiastic. As soon as he heard her voice he began to build around it, and all the first recordings were on that basis. On that very first test record he noted Sara's unique voice and knew the results were going to be wonderful. He brought the Carters before the microphone again, giving them instructions based upon his reactions to the test record. He asked them what they wanted to record next.

Doc remembers being surprised. He thought it was just going to be like the Brunswick session, where they were rushed in, sang two songs, and rushed out. Unlike the Brunswick fellow who did not know what to say about their music, Mr. Peer was excited, and looked like he would keep them there all day. During the day he even brought in some cookies and iced tea. Any song they wanted to do seemed to be fine with him.

Behind this courteous exterior was a man of acute business sense. He knew what would sell in rural areas, and he had the genuine article in his recording studio.

Doc asked if they could sing "Little Log Cabin by the Sea," and Peer readily agreed. He gave them another signal, and Maybelle played the instrumental introduction, which established the driving rhythm persisting through the song. Sara's crystalline voice rang out as she sang a tale of home, mother, and the blessed Bible that guided the family through life's storms. Doc and Maybelle joined in on the second and fourth lines and harmonized. This pattern was followed throughout the song. Ralph Peer was amazed at the driving energy they achieved in the song. He had heard nothing quite like it before. Certainly, he had been exposed to similar musical styles in his recording expeditions. But the Carter Family had polish and conviction as they praised that precious Bible, and sang of the reassurance of its message.

Maybelle took the first instrumental break, backed up by vigorous chording on Sara's Autoharp. Ralph Peer was totally unprepared for Maybelle Carter's work on the guitar and was amazed by the intense musical energy which these two women produced from only two instruments. He listened spellbound to Maybelle's bass melody-line, worried only that his equipment would be too insensitive to record it adequately. Ralph Peer was impressed by the religious message. It was obvious to him that they lived the precepts in their song. This impression was reinforced when the family sang the last verse. The lyrics reflect the promise in the Bible of life after death.

This was the kind of material which would have great sales appeal in the rural regions. You could not simply mouth platitudes and attract these people. In matters of religion and spiritual faith they were experts, and bogus articles would not move them. The Carter Family was quite another matter.

Ralph Peer had never heard "Little Log Cabin by the Sea" before this recording date. This may be difficult to understand today, when a new song can be known all over the country within a week. Now a producer can know every song thoroughly before attempting a rehearsal. For Peer, every rural song, for the most part, was a fresh experience, and he listened to them with an open ear.

The song gave him an image, and he knew it to be a powerful one for the rural audience. You saw it all so clearly—the weather-stained cabin overlooking the ocean, an aged mother reading the Bible by the light of a kerosene lantern, and a fierce storm on the ocean. In the midst of this tableau, there is the knowledge that faith, charity, and hope knit the fabric of life together.

According to the ledger sheets of Victor, the next song they recorded that day was "Poor Orphan Child." Sara sang it with a genuine, heart-felt style, as the experience of having her parents die gave her a feeling for orphaned children. No matter how hard the relatives tried, the orphan could never receive the same love from kinfolk as she could from her own mother and father. Ralph Peer had no knowledge of Sara's past, but he remembers being struck by the lyrics of "Poor Orphan Child," and the sincere emotion with which she rendered the song.

These songs were the literature of the mountains. They recorded eloquently the joys, concerns, and sorrows of the life of the people. Although the people of the mountains were inured to hardship, the plight of the orphan child was taken seriously. The child must be clothed and fed in a community which labors hard for its livelihood. The hearts of the people went out for the orphan, seeing his care as a test of their Christian charity.

The next song they recorded that day expressed a theme common in their repertoire. Its title was "Storms Are on the Ocean." The loved one has left his native land for a country unimaginable, and far away. Some scholars have asserted that these lyrics, expressing sentiments so common in the entire rural repertoire, unconsciously mourn the loss of rural cohesion. The spreading of industrial change into the South, as we have seen earlier, dissolved the isolation of rural folk in an incredibly short time. Many other Carter Family songs—such as "A Distant Land to Roam," "I'll Be Home Some Day," and "I Have No One to Love Me (but the Sailor on the Deep Blue Sea)"—reflect this state of affairs. Men and women were constantly leaving their homes in order to seek their fortunes elsewhere. But these new lands offered only worldly wealth. They could not eradicate the longing for home, or the loss of roots.

The next song recorded was "Single Girl, Married Girl," which was to become one of the Carter Family's most popular songs. Years later Sara remembered this song as the highlight of the session. Ralph Peer especially liked it and asked them to record it twice—a practice almost unheard of at that time, when there was no tape, and takes were not expected to be perfect. Peer thought the harmony could be somewhat de-emphasized. This would serve to highlight Sara's voice and Maybelle's accompaniment. Most country music buffs today would agree that Peer accomplished just this.

The last song during that session was "Wandering Boy," which echoed the themes of rural loneliness and travel to strange lands. It evoked the image of a mother left behind in the hills, thinking of her son who has traveled to a distant land. She waits for him and hopes for his return; she remembers her old rocking chair and her heart is sad; and she prays God will keep him and eventually bring him home.

The session was over. The songs the Carters had sung reflected the truth of their environment, told of its poverty, hardship, loneliness, and disappointment. But their art served to transcend these sorrows and would help others to overcome their own troubles. Ralph Peer realized this as the record session ended. Giving them their seventy-five dollars—they were shocked to receive so much—he signed them to a five-year exclusive contract with Victor. He told them the company would be in touch with them when they wanted them to make records again.

Jimmie Rodgers had been recorded the day before, and would record again the day after the Carters left the city, thus sealing Bristol's place in the history of country music.

Maybelle remembered leaving Bristol immediately afterward, picking up Gladys and baby Joe on the street, and piling into the muddy Model T for the trip back to Maces Spring. Driving along they nibbled what was left of the sandwiches. Their experience of that day was really no different for them than performing before a church audience, for example. In fact Sara later testified that, for her, it was easier than singing before an audience. "With an audience, you're always thinking about pleasing them. But making a record is different. You just go in and do your best. That's all we ever did."

At the time the session did not make a great impression upon them. Doc was pleased that Mr. Peer liked the group's singing. He did not fully realize what the contract he had signed could mean to them. Maybelle went back to her cabin in Poor Valley and was pleased to hear that the railroad had transferred Eck back to Bristol, and that he would be spending more time at home. Sara was glad to return to her daily occupations. Together she and Doc helped raise money for repairs on the Mount Vernon Methodist Church. When labor was needed Doc cut down some trees and hauled the logs and timber to the church site.

They had no indication of the phenomenal popularity their records would have. But as time went on, the requests for personal appearances began to increase so fast that even Doc was taken by surprise. None of them had realized that the records would immediately make them well-known in the area.

Original Carter Family. Sara with Autoharp, A.P., and Maybelle with guitar. *Left:* Original Carter Family. Early years as professionals, Maybelle, A.P., and Sara *seated.*

Original Carter Family radio performers, 193 Maybelle's children, *seat left to right,* Helen, Ani and June. *Standing left right,* A.P., Jeanett "Brother Bill" (radio a nouncer in Del Rio, Texa Sara, and Maybelle. *Belo* Maybelle and the Cart Sisters, June, Anita, ar Helen. "Grand O Opry"—Probably in the la forties.

"Grand Ole Opry"—Probably early fifties. *Left to right*, Anita, Hank Snow, June, and Maybelle. *Left:* June Carter, adding a touch of comedy to the act—Opry days.

Helen, Maybelle, and June—1961.

Mother Maybelle seated, backed up by her musical daughters, *left to right*, June, Anita, and Helen—1965.

Portrait of Sara. *Below:* June Carter Cash performing with her husband, Johnny. "The Johnny Cash Show" on television—1971.

# 7

# A New Horizon

*We are here we must confess*
*Just to bring you happiness,*
*We hope to please you more or less*
*So how do you do?*

Doc did not return to Bristol for at least two months after the August recording session. The work on the new church wing was taking much of his time, and he was beginning to travel into the middle of the state to sell fruit trees again. The fall of 1927 saw an increase in activity, but very little increase in money, as far as the Carters were concerned. There was simply a lot of work to be done, as there always had been, and always would be.

Sara and Maybelle were involved with a more important event. Eck Carter had just been transferred back to Bristol when Maybelle's labor pains began. Everyone who knows Maybelle Carter discerns a "touch of class" in this pioneer of country music. Her open, innocent face contrasts with her piercing, pale-blue eyes. Hers is a face with strength, the face of a woman who has seen good times and bad. As June Carter, her daughter, has said. "There is something very special" about Maybelle Carter.

Less than a month and a half after cutting her first record at the age of seventeen, Maybelle began feeling labor pains. Eck went on foot to his parents' house. "I don't remember the trip," Eck recalled. "I just remember leaving Maybelle and arriving at the folks' place. I was so nervous the trip is a blank."

Mollie Carter returned on foot with Eck and Sara, who happened to be visiting at the time. Maybelle and her husband lived in a one-room cabin. The kitchen was built as a lean-to against the side of the house. It was there she gave birth to Helen Carter. Mollie Carter was the midwife, and Maybelle went through the delivery without the aid of an aspirin, or the services of a doctor.

More exciting news was to follow. Doc had to go to Bristol to deliver a load of trees for the nursery. During the lunch break he stopped in to see Cecil McClister at the record shop. Cecil's face brightened as Doc entered. He left the counter and extended his hand—Doc had his hand shaken with such force it shocked him.

What was going on? Telling Doc to wait for a moment, he disappeared into the back of the shop and returned with a record in a brown sleeve.

"What is it?" Doc asked. Cy handed him the disk. The label read "The Carter Family." Around the bottom was printed the title of the song: "The Weeping Willow Tree." On the other side of the record was "Single Girl, Married Girl." Cy said that Mr. Peer had asked him to give Doc the record.

Doc laughed. He did not have a record player. They played the new record on the demonstration phonograph in the shop window. As he put it down on the platter Cy remarked that Doc was lucky Mr. Peer had sent him a record—there were no other copies in the county. The shop had received two hundred the month before, and they had all been sold! Doc could not believe it. He knew enough to realize that a sale like that was unusual.

Mr. Peer was quite excited about it, Cy believed. He showed Doc an enthusiastic letter from Peer reporting that the Carter Family record was doing well in all areas of the South. In Atlanta they had already sold two thousand copies. That meant money in royalties should be coming soon.

The record itself was no surprise to Doc: he had heard all the songs played back to him in the recording session. But it was strange to stand in a shop and hear the group's music coming out of a beautiful mahogany cabinet.

He rode back to Maces Spring in a happy daze!

When Doc arrived home, two invitations to perform were waiting for him. A church wanted the Carter Family to perform on a Sunday, and a group of people were having a barn dance and wanted the Carters to sing. The letters had been dropped off at the cabin by private messengers, since the rural postal delivery was extremely uncertain.

These two letters do not exist. Only one such letter has survived, and its tone seems to be typical.

Dear Sara and all,

to night I will drop you a few lines as I am thinking of you  hope this will find you all well and getting along fine.

This leaves us all well and getting along all OK.

We have been gardening to beat the band for the past week.

Sara the . . . lodge here has ask me again to write you all a bout giving an Entertainment here. I wrote you once and never had an answer perhaps you didnt get my letter. So they ask me to write again. they want to put this on in the court house at Wise they think we could make more money as the folks turn out better At Wise than they do here. We will be willing to have what ever you all think is right, and we will do all the Advertsing  Write us what you will do. Where you will come are not and what persent you give to us let me no by monday if you can. Of course we will do all the advertising and get the building and Every thing. All you will have to do is come over and make the music. So be sure and let me no by monday if you can.

your friend,
Laura James

Most of their personal appearances were arranged in this way. Shortly after the first record came out, Doc decided to print up fliers to help local groups advertise the show. There is one example of a Carter Family flier which has survived:

L O O K!
Victor Artist
A. P. C A R T E R
AND
THE CARTER FAMILY
will give
a
musical program
at ______________________
________________________
on ______________________

________________________
The program is morally good
Admission: 15 and 25 Cents
________________________
A. P. Carter, Maces Spring

It is not known whether Doc, Sara, and Maybelle agreed to perform at the request of the church or the barn dance, but if they did, their appearance would have followed their general, informal pattern. When they decided to play, Doc immediately took over all the advance work for the group. His hopes for a professional career were becoming a reality, and he wanted to involve himself in every aspect of it.

He sent ahead some fliers on which the group could write the place and time of the Carters' performance. On the appointed date, the Carters piled into an automobile for the trip. (By 1928 they purchased a Model T especially for these expeditions.) When they arrived, a crowd probably would be milling around the front of the church or barn where the show was to be held. The show would run from about seven-thirty until nine-thirty. Sara and Maybelle sold the tickets themselves; pushing through the crowd and exchanging greetings, they would take up a position by the door of the hall. Doc would go inside and see that all the preparations had been made. Then the crowd would be admitted—they would stand around chatting until the show began. It was the Carters' practice to mingle with the crowd until it was time for them to go on stage.

The platform might be nothing more than ten or so planks resting on top of two large sawhorses. It was a rarity to have electric lights in those years, and they usually performed in the glow of flickering kerosene lanterns. When all of the people were seated either

Doc or Sara would step forward to call the audience to order, and to sing a musical welcome.

Doc called out to the audience, "How do you do?" They echoed him in a loud hello of their own. Then they sang "Keep on the Sunny Side," which they had made their performing theme song. Then Doc, who served as MC, stepped to the front of the stage and introduced each member of the group.

He would introduce Sara first, and then his sister-in-law, Maybelle, and then any other friend or relative who happened to be singing along with them that night. In the early days, after their first recording sessions, they would usually perform alone. As time went on, their children and friends often joined them.

After this brief preparation, the Carter Family would begin to sing with a minimum of fuss. After a song ended, and the applause ended, Doc would say, "Thank you, thank you. Our next number will be. . . ." When the song was not known by most of the audience, he told a brief story about its origins; and, if he himself had discovered it on one of his song-hunting trips, he would tell a longer tale. If the song was on a record, they would casually mention that fact. During intermission the group sold song folios which they had printed—but photographs or records were never hawked.

"We could have sold records," Maybelle remembers, "but all of us felt about those performances just like you would feel about visiting some friends. They could buy our records elsewhere. They came to see us in person, and we came to please them."

Maybelle and Sara usually sat on two straight-backed chairs while they performed. It was Doc's habit to stand behind them. As the evening progressed, he would begin to wander about the stage, sometimes leaving it altogether in the middle of a song. Doc was always nervous, even as a young man. This gave his singing its distinctive style, the "tear in his voice" of which Virgie Carter Hobbs has spoken. Doc's mother always believed this quality of voice came from the stormy weather on the night of his birth!

An informal atmosphere prevailed during the Carter Family performances. The Family sang comedy songs on occasion, but in the early years there was no comedy during the show—it was devoted entirely to music. They would ask the audience for requests, but when the performance ended there would be no encores, and the audience did not expect any. This is still a common practice among the rural folk performers of today.

If an instrument needed restringing or retuning, it would be done directly on stage between numbers. Unlike the professionals of today, they did not carry extra instruments to avoid this time-consuming task. The time taken for tuning was one of the sources for humor for comedy acts in rural performances. But the Carter Family belonged to an earlier era, and did not begin using comedy in their act until the late thirties.

The homelike atmosphere of these performances was also shown by the Carters' willingness to give two or three shows if the crowds were too large to fit into the hall. This occurred frequently on occasions when the Family had expected only one performance.

After the show the Family would usually stay at the home of the person who arranged the concert. It was during these stays that intense song-swapping meetings took place. Often Maybelle would stay up way past midnight singing with their hosts, long after Doc, Sara, and the children were in bed.

Even with the increased opportunities for performing, their music still could not support them completely. Doc, naive about the music business, did not expect much of a royalty check for their first recording effort, even though he had been told it was selling well. When it came, in the astounding amount of $150, it encouraged him to think again that music might make him self-supporting. But the record companies had the upper hand in those early days of the music business, and the Carter Family, by contract, received a quarter of a cent on each record sold. The royalty checks seemed slow in coming.

In the early months of 1928 Doc was again forced to go north. The royalty check had paid off some longstanding debts, but with four mouths to feed, money was still a problem. Through the owner of the nursery, he had been in contact with a building contractor up in

Detroit who offered him a job at high wages. Doc had become an expert carpenter during the twenties and he was hired to work in Detroit.

Sara was against the trip, but there was very little choice. Work was becoming extremely difficult to find in Virginia; the Depression had hit, and the prosperity of the late twenties had faded. Some people were saying hard times were here to stay, and Doc had the responsibility to take any good job offered him.

There were other workers in the area going to Detroit at the same time, and the employer sent a truck down for them. Doc arrived in a bitterly cold Detroit in the early weeks of February. He was assigned to do interior work on a number of apartment houses and slept in a rooming house with the other workmen from his area. In the rooming house he came into close contact with blacks for the first time in his life.

It was a pivotal point in Doc Carter's musical education. Contrary to common assumption, not all parts of the South are inhabited by large numbers of blacks. In fact, A. P. Carter's part of the country was known to have definite northern sympathies during the Civil War. The mountain dwellers were fiercely independent, and they could not make much sense out of any defense of slavery.

The blacks did not live in Doc's boardinghouse. They were servants helping the landlady, or workmen on the various jobs to which Doc was assigned. Doc had seen perhaps three or four blacks in his life. Now he found himself working next to them. He watched them with fascination.

Music seemed as important to them as it was to Doc. They sang constantly as they worked, and it seemed to make the work go easier for them. Of course, they were not hundreds of miles from home—for the most part they lived in Detroit. But most of them had recently moved from the deep South, and there were feelings of loneliness in their hearts. He felt it in their music. There was a quiet but strong undercurrent of sadness, even in the most throbbing of their rhythms. Doc listened carefully and sometimes after work he would scribble down the words of the work songs he remembered. The black music opened up a new world of harmony, cadence, and rhythm.

Other than this new musical influence, however, the months in Detroit were lonely, worse perhaps than his time in Indianapolis. Now Doc had three children and often thought of Gladys, Jeanette, and Joe; he prayed to God that they would be kept safe and healthy until his return. He spent as little money as possible, sending almost all of his weekly wage home to Sara.

In May 1928 a letter arrived at the rooming house which released Doc from his exile. It was a letter from Sara enclosing a letter from Ralph Peer. It asked the

Carter Family to take a train up north to Camden, New Jersey. Mr. Peer wanted to make some more records. He enclosed a money order for $100 to cover expenses. Sara had cashed it and sent Doc twenty dollars with the admonition to "come right home." He was glad to obey!

Late Monday night May 7, Maybelle, Sara, and Doc boarded a northbound train in Bristol. Maybelle and Sara had never been on a train before, and neither of them had been farther than fifty miles from Scott County. They were overwhelmed by the industrialized north with its dirt and noise. During a change of trains in the Philadelphia railroad station, they experienced the crush of a typical big-city crowd. It made Maybelle, in particular, especially nervous.

Peer sent a driver and car to meet them, and they were taken to a good Camden hotel. They were struck by the elegance of the rooms and the luxury of having hot and cold running water. Even Doc's experience in the North had denied him this pleasure. Both the Salvation Army mission and the boardinghouse had provided only porcelain water pitchers and washbasins.

May 9 was a day of even more unexpected sights. Late in the morning Ralph Peer ushered them into Victor's main recording studio. Peer opened a metal door and they entered a room surrounded on all sides by double-paned windows. Behind the windows they could see a great bank of gauges and dials; men who had strange devices perched on top of their heads were staring at the Carters. Doc whispered to Sara that the head-sets were "earphones," a bit of information he had picked up from Peer during the last recording session.

Although all of them were somewhat awed by their technological surroundings, they were quickly able to take their places and tune up when Peer gave them the signal. It was another example of their innate professionalism, and Peer was impressed again.

It was to be seen later as an historic occasion. (In 1965, *Billboard,* the industry journal, called it "The Two Days that Shook the Country Music World.") The Bristol session had established their talent in Ralph Peer's mind, but the Camden session set the Carters up for great commercial success. Peer had been satisfied with their talent but felt that their extensive repertoire could be used to greater advantage. On that day in 1928, Peer sat with them in the studios for two hours. They talked and went over some of the songs the Carters knew. They sang him a few bars of each tune; he noted the titles of the songs he especially liked.

It was during this session that Ralph Peer showed his true genius. His first meeting with the Carters could be called fortuitous. In the second session, however, it was Peer's direction which contributed to the quality of the recordings. Although he was not (at this time) a country-music expert, Peer had an intuitive grasp of the Carters' commercial potential. During the airing of their repertoire, Peer selected 12 songs which were to form the core of the 250 Carter records they made in their lifetime.

On May 9 only two songs were recorded. The first was "Meet Me by Moonlight, Alone." This selection typifies the nonreligious portion of the Carter Family's work. It is a lonesome tale of a forsaken girl who is driven from her home by cruel parents. She desires to meet her lover by moonlight, but he is away, over the ocean.

The next selection was "Little Darling, Pal of Mine." It has been recorded by innumerable country artists since 1928. (One of the most notable versions was Gene Autry's.) This is one of the Carter Family's most heartbreaking songs. Its lyric might seem overblown today, but it obviously touched many people. At the time of the record's release, block-long lines formed outside of record shops, with every person waiting to buy this record. The heartbroken lover in the song longed for only three things—casket, shroud, and grave—it was a sentiment popular among rural youth of the time. The Carter Family's skillful embodiment of this feeling helped to make the record their first million-seller. The record was to make them famous all over the United States.

May 10, 1928, was the marathon session. On this day the Carter Family recorded ten songs. One of these was "Keep on the Sunny Side," their theme song, and second most-popular release of their career. Wherever they appeared, on radio, stage, or barn dance, the optimistic words of this song could be heard.

The other selections included two spirituals which formed a central part of their repertoire: "Anchored in Love," and "River of Jordan." Several songs had never been recorded before this session: "Forsaken Love," "Wildwood Flower" (which Maybelle often sang later in her career), "John Hardy, John Hardy," and "I Ain't Goin' to Work Tomorrow" (a humorous song which featured Maybelle's lead guitar).

Later that night the family boarded the train for home with high hopes. Peer was enthusiastic as the session ended and told them they could expect to make a good bit of money from the records they had made. He gave them $150 as an advance on the royalties to come. This was probably the most money the Carter Family had been paid for a performance up to that time. Although it was not a large payment, the family, having been inured to poverty, saw it as a windfall.

While they all continued to work at rural occupations, these chores did not fill the major part of their lives after the historic 1928 record date. Music now was their true vocation, and this was a matter of some pride, as well as a small measure of guilt. The Carters did not live in a region which understood how one could properly claim to make a living from music. Although music was a part of their culture, it was as free as the sweet air of the mountains. The Carter Family began to live with a certain measure of anxiety and adjustment to their new role. Doc quit selling fruit trees and did only occasional carpentry. Most of his time was now spent promoting singing tours, collecting songs, and rehearsing with the group.

Maybelle was forced to move away from Poor Valley. Eck was transferred by the railroad again in 1929, and the young couple moved to Bluefield, West Virginia. Just before the move, Maybelle gave birth to her second child. Mollie Carter again served as midwife. The little girl was named Valerie June Carter. Eck, Maybelle, and their two children remained in West Virginia for two years. In 1931 the family moved to Washington, D.C.

The beginning of the Depression saw the Carter Family break up as a kind of musical collective, a group which lived and made music together. But the commercial career of the group was by no means ended. Rehearsals were difficult to arrange, but the Carters relied on an extensive repertoire, and they were not really needed. They kept in touch by mail. Doc would inform Maybelle of concert dates, which she always made an effort to attend.

Even with record sales in the millions, their royalties remained modest and could not completely support them. If they wished to make their living making music, they would have to sing at more concert dates. To an interviewer in the late sixties, Maybelle admitted, "We were never rich. Our music just got us by. But don't forget, in the Depression that was enough. We were lucky compared to most." Stars of their magnitude today would easily earn a half-million dollars a year. Even contemporaries of the Carters earned more; Jimmie Rodgers is a prominent example. The financial success of Rodgers could be attributed to the expert legal and financial advice he received. The Carter Family simply did not have access to such help—they had a homespun career. All of their promotion was done by Doc himself, who always charged fifteen or twenty-five cents for admission. He did not realize the group could have made at least $150 a week on the vaudeville circuit.

When Jimmie Rodgers met the Carter Family, it was an unusual occasion. In the late spring of 1931 Maybelle received a telegram from Ralph Peer asking her to meet the rest of the group in Louisville, Kentucky. Peer had arranged a recording session with Rodgers, Victor's most popular artist. Eck was able to get a few days off, and he and Maybelle headed west from Washington, D.C., where they were then living.

Sara, Doc, and Maybelle came together at the railroad station and took a taxicab to the temporary recording studio. Passing a large, white Packard parked on the street outside, they walked into the warehouse-recording studio, not prepared for what was to follow.

There was a crowd of people milling about inside the warehouse, blocking the narrow corridors. The people were oblivious to the entrance of the Carter Family, barely moving to let them pass. The blue haze of cigar smoke hung in the air. Maybelle remembers hearing a persistent cough in the distance as they pushed past the men. Suddenly Ralph Peer appeared and ushered them into a room.

It was the temporary recording studio, and Jimmie Rodgers was lying in the center of the room on a cot. He was covered up to the neck in quilts and he coughed continually. Four or five men stood behind the cot offering Jimmie drinks and handkerchiefs from time to time, but he impatiently waved them all away. They were introduced, Jimmie Rodgers waved his retinue back, urging the shy Carter Family forward. The other men edged up to the glass walls of the recording studio as the Carters and Jimmie Rodgers shook hands. The royalty of the newly burgeoning country-music business were conferring. The men from the North could not really understand the meaning of the moment. They may have thought they were witnessing the meeting of equals.

Artistically, the Carter Family and Jimmie Rodgers were on the same plane. In other areas of life, however, there was a great gap between them. Although both had rural roots, Rodgers veered from his background. His fame and large income had made him a thorough professional. The Carters, on the other hand, had remained closer to their culture and stood in awe of Jimmie. They must have wondered how Rodgers had managed to come into such wealth, when their musical success had only brought them a small amount of money.

Their professionalism was intact, however. The Carters swallowed whatever awe and uneasiness they might have felt. Peer motioned the other men out of the studio and asked the Carters and Rodgers what songs they would sing. There is a question as to which songs they recorded on that day. Some would have it that the "Wildwood Flower" and Jimmie's "Blue Yodel" were recorded—with Rodgers singing, and the Carters providing harmony and instrumental accompaniment. (A complete discography of the Carter Family does not exist, and no one can give supporting data, such as release or master numbers.)

When the recording studio was cleared, it soon became obvious that Rodgers was much too ill to play his guitar. His coughing was almost constant, the result of an advanced case of tuberculosis. Maybelle remembers three doctors being present, watching anxiously from the control booth, and pressing their faces up against the glass at every cough. Before the session could begin, the doctors treated him and sprayed various medicines into his mouth. Rodgers listened intently as one doctor advised him not to strain his voice, and another was bold enough to order him not to record at all.

Ralph Peer interceded and suggested that Maybelle Carter play lead guitar instead of Rodgers. The doctors agreed to this compromise. Maybelle protested that she could not play like Jimmie—he had his own distinctive style. Record buyers would surely know that somebody else was playing. But Peer was adamant. He assured Maybelle that she could do it. He reminded her that she had imitated Jimmie's playing style (as a joke) at the Carters' earlier recording session.

The four songs were recorded. Maybelle later said, "I had to play like him, you know, so everybody would think it was him. But it was me. And to this day very few people have asked me about it."

After the session Rodgers was so ill he was taken to his hotel room to rest. They were never to see him again before he died. But the visit gave all of them, and especially Doc, a taste of the rewards of professionalism. The Carter Family's career picked up momentum after that visit.

A third recording session was arranged in Camden,

during which "Little Moses" was recorded. This, perhaps, was their finest hymn—it was popularized during the sixties by Joan Baez. A fourth recording session was scheduled in New York. Their records began to be listed in the Sears Roebuck catalog, and this exposure accelerated their record sales.

Doc expanded his tour promotion, deciding to perform at least once every two weeks. "The money is there," he told Sara. "There's no reason for me to do other work when we can earn money with our music." Although the Carter Family rarely made appearances more than 150 miles away from Scott County, the group began touring. They became pioneers in that erratic way of life which was to prove the undoing of so many country-music stars in the years to come.

Doc no longer relied on invitations from potential audiences. After 1931 he began to mail fliers to an extensive list of names which he had been compiling since 1927. His solicitations produced results, and the Carter Family performance schedule was constantly full. The pressure became so great that Maybelle was urged to move back to Scott County three months before her patient husband could wangle a transfer from Washington to Bristol. The group now needed to be together so that they could make most of the concert dates. Some audiences, up to the time of Eck's transfer, were making do with Doc and Sara. Often it was just too much to expect Maybelle to come. At their only recorded trip north (to Boston in late 1931) Doc and Sara were forced to perform alone. It was after this event that Doc persuaded Maybelle to return to Scott County.

Too much money was involved, Doc Carter later recalled. There were hard times, and when one could make money, it was foolish not to. Doc was thinking of more than his own pocketbook. He joined the congregation of the Mount Vernon Methodist Church in 1930. As the group's fame and record sales increased, Doc voluntarily promised a tithe of thirty percent to the church. In late 1931 he increased his share to fifty percent.

As long as the Carters invested their lives in their own career, their income would increase. As Doc knew, there was money to be made, and the group had to force themselves into an unfamiliar routine in order to make it. Up to the time of their meeting with Jimmie Rodgers, the idea of a musical career had still seemed slightly unreal to them. But that experience, and other realizations of their fame—the constant flow of fan mail, for one thing—compelled them into steady touring.

The performances became weekly affairs. As time went on they began performing two and three times a week. Maybelle's return to Scott County undoubtedly sparked this increasing pace. Doc visited with them once or twice a month. He would pull out a notebook and show them the letters he had received confirming the month's concert dates. Doc estimated the time needed to travel to each location and informed Maybelle of the time he would pick her up at her cabin. At the appointed time, Doc would drive up to Maybelle's place in the Model A the Carters had purchased for their tours. Then would follow a hard stretch of traveling over rough, two-lane blacktops to towns, cities, and hamlets in four states. They confined their tours to Virginia, West Virginia, North Carolina, and Tennessee, and occasionally they ventured into Maryland and Pennsylvania. More extensive trips could not be taken since the amount of money they received for each performance was still modest.

The easy, relaxed informality of their early appearances quickly disappeared in their effort to blend a professional life with a traditional mountain way of living. This was not easy. The concert date would be played, but they could not remain behind to chat with the audience when the concert was over. Nor could they mingle with the crowd before the performance began. They had to leave immediately for home.

Soon Doc was arranging performances back to back, and the group was forced to leave one concert immediately for another concert. Maybelle and Sara objected; the children could not be brought along on every trip, and they could not be without their parents forever. Doc loved this kind of professional life more than the others did. It was his desire for a full-fledged professional career which conflicted with Sara's equally ardent wish for a normal home life. She was hardly seeing her children any more. And on top of that, Doc began to dictate to the others, urging them into accepting concert dates when Sara and Maybelle had no energy to go on.

Besides the tours, recording sessions had to be fitted into the schedule. Maybelle and Eck disliked the separations required by the many trips. Eck asked his older brother to moderate the activity of the Carter Family, but at first Doc refused. The conflict between career and home-life took its toll.

In 1933 Doc and Sara were separated. She moved back to Copper Creek with the children, leaving Doc to live alone in the cabin he had built with his own hands. They were never to live under the same roof again. After much prayer and reflection they had decided it was God's will that they try to live fulfilling lives apart from each other. They were both good people, and life went on. Maybelle too was affected. She cared deeply about the two other members of the group, having known them both since her childhood. But in the end she could not bury her own individuality for the sake of the group. She began to demand that the touring be cut down and her insistence on change probably saved the group from splitting up earlier than it ultimately did.

For the first time in some years, the group was now back in Scott County, and they continued to rehearse and make music together, even when they were not performing. In later years, all members of the group frankly admitted that things went better after the separation than before. Their personal and professional lives could now be separated. With the continuing increase in the sales of their records, all of them could now afford to live entirely on royalties. If their lives were not luxurious, the royalties kept them free from want during the worst of the Depression.

# 8

## On the Air!

*Radio touched almost all aspects of life among the common people—it made country music a nationwide medium.*

The separation of Doc and Sara Carter sent shock waves through the world of country music. Those not close to the situation thought it would precipitate the breakup of the group. In order to heal the emotional wounds, the Carter Family temporarily stopped making music together. Maybelle began to learn classical music on the guitar during this period. It is not known whether Sara worked on her music during this time, but she labored diligently to establish a home for her children in Copper Creek.

The initial years of their professional career had taken a great toll on them. The grind of traveling to concert appearances was wearing all of them down. Doc, Sara, and Maybelle needed a respite from the demands of their career. To gain it, they temporarily suspended their activities together. For a full year they did not perform in public. Only one record date was scheduled during that period, and only four songs were recorded. But there was very little thought of abandoning the musical career which had given them pleasure and recognition—so long as that career was kept within bounds.

"I had wanted to sing all my life, and being able to make money from it seemed the best thing of all," Doc later said of those times. "But I didn't realize the price you had to pay for it. I had a private life too, and I didn't want to throw that away." Although the family's musical career slowed down at this time, they had income from their past releases and they could afford to go back to the life of the mountains. This was the only way they could maintain their values. Doc started serving part-time as choral director for a number of churches in the area, and he began working again as a part-time carpenter. "Working with my hands made time go faster," Doc later recalled, "and I could always sing to myself while hammering nails."

Maybelle had children to raise and new kinds of music to learn. On March 31, 1933, she was introduced to the methods of modern childbirth. In a newer and larger cabin, wholly financed by record royalties, she gave birth to her youngest, Anita. Mother-in-law Mollie Carter assisted her again, but this time Dr. Meade from Mendota, Virginia was also present. It was lucky he was—this was Maybelle's most difficult delivery. The two children were sent away for the night. When they returned they found a fat, ten-and-one-half-pound baby girl. "Everybody was worried about mother for awhile," June Carter recalled, "because her lips were blue, and she was pale as chalk. And daddy stayed by the bedside for days. But mother got better real soon, and Anita cried and cried, getting fatter by the minute."

In 1935 the Carter Family's contract with Victor ended. Over the past three years, Victor's attitude toward the group had begun to irritate Doc. He still managed the Carters' business affairs, and his opinions had weight. Tour! Perform before more live audiences! Tours help sales! Doc resented such demands and viewed them as intrusions into their private lives. He had learned his lesson and was having none of it. Despite the separation the group had maintained its relationship by cutting down on its obligations. It confused and frustrated A. P. Carter that folks could not understand this.

It was inevitable, then, that Doc would sign a contract with another record company, although Ralph Peer still controlled all publication rights to most of their songs. (His business continues to hold these rights to this day.) In late 1935 Doc, Sara, and Maybelle signed a contract with the American Record Company. By this time Peer had left Victor also. He still continued to advise Doc about the group's business affairs. Carter discs were issued until 1940 under such labels as Banner, Columbia, Conqueror, Coral Decca, Melotone, Montogomery Ward, Okeh, Oriole, Perfect, Romeo, and Vocalion. Doc had arranged a significant amount of new material during this period, and record buyers were treated to this expansion in the Carter Family repertoire. It now included a number of new songs, mostly written by Doc and Maybelle, as well as a variety of British traditional ballads. "Black Jack David" and "Sinking in the Lonesome Sea" were especially popular with the record-buying public.

In 1935 they expanded their touring. Sara was now more willing to perform, and Maybelle was beginning to miss the stage. One day they asked Doc to schedule more appearances, and he was pleased to do so. Their record sales grew as their personal appearances increased, and by 1937 they no longer had financial problems—although, as Maybelle has recalled, they were never rich.

These new tours interested people in the booming radio business in the Carter Family. During the thirties there was a great rivalry between the radio and the record industries. (It was not until 1948 that commercially released discs were allowed to be played over network stations.) In those days network radio, and even the independent stations, relied upon live concerts and shows. After 1936 the Carter Family began to appear on several barn-dance shows which were broadcast throughout the southeast. However, the Carters never appeared regularly. It was "Dr." John Romulus Brinkley, self-proclaimed doctor of medicine, politician, and pioneer of the radio medium, who brought them to a larger audience as "regular radio performers."

Brinkley was an entrepreneur with imagination. His radio station, identified with call letters XERA, was located near the Mexican border in Del Rio, Texas. With a powerful transmitter and a directional antenna, XERA could broadcast to wide areas of the South. (It was said that folks living near the transmitter could pick up broadcasts on their fillings.) Radio touched almost all aspects of life among the common people—it made country music a nationwide medium. Although phonograph records were widely distributed, one needs money to buy them. Radio was as free as the air, and the sounds XERA broadcast across the continent were a potent force in shaping the modern musical forms of the nation.

Listeners to XERA, as well as listeners to the other border stations, responded most to hillbilly and gospel music. By 1936 this kind of music was almost a border-station exclusive. Many performers who were known because of their recordings were hired to broadcast "live" on a regular basis. Don Howard, who served as program director for Brinkley in the mid-thirties, was a pioneer in this type of programming. The station had tried all sorts of music, but Howard switched almost entirely to country music.

During this time Howard was contacted by the Consolidated Royal Chemical Corporation of Chicago. They were attracted by the wide coverage of XERA and became a regular advertiser. Howard suggested that they hire hillbilly groups and bring them to Texas to perform on a "Consolidated Chemical Hour." This suggestion struck a responsive chord in Harry O'Neill, Royal Chemical's advertising manager.

O'Neill, a red-cheeked, rotund man, was a pioneer in radio promotion. His client Consolidated Chemical was the first pharmaceutical company to advertise its products over the air. Thanks to O'Neill's advertising efforts products like Peruna, an anti-cold tonic, and Kolor-Bak, a hair tint, sold extremely well in rural areas. In the early days of radio a single sponsor would finance the whole program, so the format of the show was all-important to the sponsoring company. O'Neill experimented with many formats before he finally hit upon country music. He later admitted he didn't like it much at first, but it sure did sell Kolor-Bak!

Harry O'Neill hired many of the most popular hillbilly groups to broadcast over stations throughout the country. He would hire an announcer for each group to accompany them at their performances. This announcer became identified with the format in the minds of the audience. The informal atmosphere which appealed to the rural audience was maintained by the announcer; he would speak in a homespun style, always trying to set the audience at ease. Consolidated Chemical never gave a direct pitch for its products. Listeners were invited to send in a box top from one of the products in order to receive a free Bible, or other gift, in the return mail. A mailing list was created in this way, and sales were stimulated. Each time a farmer sent in one box top, it was worth fifty cents to Consolidated, O'Neill estimated.

Howard and O'Neill corresponded, and Howard suggested that Consolidated hire the Carter Family, one of his personal favorites. "I knew they had been on the radio," he remembers, "but I never heard them. They weren't on the air as often as some other groups, and I told Harry they would pull in a great audience. Everybody in the country liked them."

In the late summer of 1936 Ralph Peer placed a long-distance call to A. P. Carter (who had installed a telephone in his cabin by this time). Consolidated had made a tremendous offer and he was quite excited about it. Peer felt that the group just should not pass up the opportunity. He knew of their wish to relax for a while and was afraid they would refuse. But Doc was as excited as Peer hoped he would be. Doc couldn't believe anybody would pay anybody that kind of money just to sing on the radio!

The money does not seem like much today. The Carter Family was to receive seventy-five dollars per person each week and a paid six-month vacation. In addition, all travel expenses would be paid. Doc jumped at it and did not have to convince the others. Maybelle was very happy and excited about performing on the radio. Sara said that, with the six-month vacation, it would be possible to move the entire family down south.

Late in September the Carter Family began a marathon automobile trip from Maces Spring to Del Rio, Texas. Doc was at the wheel of a large, four-door Chevrolet which was purchased for them by Consolidated Chemical. Sara, Jeanette, and Maybelle were with him. Maybelle left her children with Doc's youngest sister, Sylvia, who was perhaps "the unsung hero of the Carter Family," as June Carter has said. Sylvia sang with the Family on many occasions when Sara could not perform with them, and she had served as a tower of strength for her brother and his wife when they were undergoing the agonies of their separation.

Strapped to the back, along with their luggage, was Maybelle's motorcycle, which she had purchased only the year before. Eck was there to see them off in the early morning dawn, and he promised to join them in a few weeks, after he secured a leave of absence from the railroad. Their income from the contract was enough for the entire family, and they could all be together in Texas for six months out of the year.

By taking this cross-country automobile trip, the Carters were traveling in a way which was to become a tradition in the country-music field. Country-music performers have worn out ten-thousand-dollar Cadillacs in six months of touring. The lonely midnight ride from one concert date to another is a part of country-music legend.

Sara remembers the trip vividly. She and Doc tried to be friendly and the trip was relaxed. Doc wasn't in a talkative mood however, he had never driven that much before and was watching the road too much to talk. Doc, nervous as usual about getting to Texas on time, drove nearly ten hours a day. "Doc loved cars," Maybelle recalls, "and the Chevy was new and a pleasure to drive, so I guess he wanted to drive as much as he could. He would hardly ever let me take the wheel, even though he knew I was a good driver. I didn't mind the rush myself, though. I was almost as anxious to get down to Texas as he was."

Eight days after the Carters left Maces Spring, Harry Steele was on the steps of the Del Rio Grand Hotel to meet them as they drove into the small border-town. He was to be their announcer for their show, the "Consolidated Chemical Radio Hour." Doc called from a booth outside Del Rio and told Harry that they would be pulling into town in a half-hour. Steele didn't recognize them when they first drove up. It was the dustiest car he ever had seen. A tall man in blue trousers stepped out and squinted at him. It wasn't until the two women stepped out of the car that it dawned on him who they were.

On this day the Carter Family entered a new world. In Harry Steele they were meeting a thorough, urbane professional, who would be their guide through the puzzling world of radio. During the course of their career, they had always been insulated from the rigors of the high-powered music business. Their cabins in Scott County were a refuge when the music business exhausted them. During periods of personal trouble, their country background had provided a shield against the pressures which could have destroyed their lives.

In Texas they were exposed to radio's high-pressure world from the beginning. Shortly after Harry Steele had installed them in the apartment provided by Consolidated Chemical, the demands began. They were asked for a written run-down of their songs for a show to be broadcast that very night. Since the dates for their shows were written in the contract, they had to oblige. That night they sang as well on radio as they had always sung on records. Though you could see the fatigue in their faces, you couldn't hear it in the singing. They were real pros.

The frantic pace did not diminish for the first few months of their stint in Texas. The Consolidated Chemical Radio Hour was aired at 8:10 each night. The Carters were the stars and had to open and close each show with a song. There were other acts, such as other musical groups, and country-style comedians. But the Carters were the main attraction and probably sang during half of the show. Harry Steele introduced each act; at the beginning, middle, and end of the show he invited the audience to send in their box tops.

The Consolidated program lasted for two hours and it was a solid period of pure entertainment. The performers, especially the Carter Family, earned their salaries and free lodging, since they were also required to spend most of the afternoon rehearsing for the evening show. During the show a transcript disc was cut on a Presto cutter. This record would then be played over XERA in the morning, freeing the groups from producing two shows a day.

The Carters had only Sunday off, and the pace soon proved more exhausting than their tours had ever been. The pressure drove the group apart once again. They had been living separate lives; the constant association, forced by the relentless grind of the broadcast schedule, bred many conflicts. You hardly had any time to yourself, Maybelle recalled. They had to practice every afternoon and they rarely had any time off. It surely wasn't like the old times, appearing before the folks in a courthouse, or at a church dance—it was all business. There was barely time for dinner and a nap before the broadcast began.

Sara was affected too. Just months before she left for Texas, a man named Coy Bayes came into her life. He was a native of Wise County and Doc Carter's first cousin. Sara had known him for a while when she was a young girl. Coy Bayes had moved to California in his twenties, returning to Scott County to visit in 1936. He had been quite successful in the timber business in Angel's Camp, California (in the foothills of the Sierra Nevadas, an area much like the hills of his native county). He had visited Sara's place in Copper Creek, and the two of them had become friends. Sara promised to write to Coy when she left Virginia. Every day she sat down and wrote him a long letter. By the time they were broadcasting, Coy had returned to California and was writing to her regularly, too.

The constant round of broadcasts also made Sara lonely for her children back in Virginia. Having Jeanette along was a comfort, but Sara was lonesome for the quiet life back in Copper Creek. The stint in Texas was hard for Sara.

Maybelle Carter missed her husband and children, too. During the first year in Texas, Eck managed to get a leave of absence from the railroad and joined her in Del Rio a month or so after the broadcasts began. Doc was perhaps the loneliest of them all, although he had a stoic personality and never talked about his feelings while in Texas.

The Carter Family broadcasts were more successful than Consolidated had hoped. During a typical week, 25,000 box tops poured into the XERA studios. Consolidated, through Ralph Peer and Harry O'Neill, renewed the Carter's contract for another year. The broadcasts sold more Carter Family records than ever before, even though no promotion of their releases was allowed on the air. For the first time in their lives, the money was literally pouring in (by their standards). They could look forward to a six-month respite from broadcasting during which there would be no need to work. It made the hard work of broadcasting seem worthwhile.

To the Carter Family, however, money was never the prime motivation. Earning a living by making music was certainly foremost in their minds, especially for Doc and Maybelle. But the show-business bug had bitten them early, and money is rarely the most important motivation for the urge to perform. For Sara, however, a career was never as important, but she was loyal to the group—they were "family." When they left Texas after six months they were satisfied with the money they had earned. With proper husbanding, they would also be able to put some aside during their six-month vacation. For Doc, it was an opportunity to increase the support he gave to the Mount Vernon Methodist Church, and after returning to Virginia he promised to give seventy percent of his income to the church.

During the months to follow Doc stepped up his search for lyric ideas to set to music. He had more money now and could afford to travel much farther through the countryside. One of these trips was particularly interesting. It shows one of the ways in which black music influenced white culture in this country.

Through his informants, Doc had learned of an elderly, black man who knew a great many coal-mining songs. These kinds of lyrics had always interested Doc. He often heard of men killed in mining accidents and recalled many stories of coal-mining families spending their lives in degrading poverty. But he didn't have any mining songs in his repertoire and hoped to find some if he could.

At first the man was a disappointment. Doc met him on the porch of his tumbledown shack, rocking in a faded-blue rocking chair. The black man was deaf, and although he had worked in the coal mines for most of his life, he had no songs to sing. But he was a wonderful storyteller, and Doc was beguiled by him, spending the rest of the afternoon listening to his tales of the coal mines.

Just as Doc rose to leave, the old man raised his hand saying, "Wait, I just remember something you oughta see." He disappeared into his shack for a moment and came back out again through the rusty screen door, which banged and shuddered against the walls of the shack. He held up empty palms. "I thought I had somebody write the words down once, but I can't find it." It was the words to a song sung by black miners he had worked with up in West Virginia. Doc said he had been up that way, and had seen the coal miners working. This seemed to please the black man, and he smiled. "They's easy to remember," he said, "I don't know why I had them written down!" Then he settled back in his rocking chair and spoke the words. The man described the woes of the miners and colorfully referred to them as soul-blue and coal-black blues. The words struck Doc immediately. He recognized the genuine pain in these lyrics, and knew he could find the music which would fit the words perfectly. Doc later titled the song "Coal Miner's Blues."

Doc often found words which lacked music—he called them "poetry." The old man had suggested the germ of a song; Doc had only to employ the methods he had used over the years, which he calling "working up" a song. Doc was essentially functioning as a folk-music scholar, but he did not see himself in this light. His techniques, however, were quite unscholarly, because he failed to note names, places, or dates. This was the common practice of most untutored musicians in the South.

It is significant that Doc felt no reticence in accepting the lyrics from a black man. By the late thirties black forms had thoroughly permeated country music, and Doc was one of the pioneers in this process.

Maybelle rode her motorcycle often that summer. "It was the prettiest little green and white Harley you could ever hope to see," she remembered years later. Eck had a bigger, black Harley, and they began driving all over the surrounding counties on the cycles. She and her husband were riding down the county road to Gate City one hot afternoon in late August when they came upon a serious accident. A motorcycle had collided with a school bus. It was crumpled on the ground, Eck remembered. The front wheel was crushed into a ball of rubber, metal, and spokes. The crash had thrown it one hundred feet down the road. The motorcycle was smoldering and charred black, but the cyclist was in worse shape. The police had to cover him with a tarp. The bus only had a little dent in its side.

The scene bothered Maybelle much more than Eck. They drove back home immediately, having lost the taste for traveling that day. When they got home Maybelle swore off her motorcycle and convinced Eck to do the same. "It was the thought of June riding behind me, with her tiny hand clutched around my waist," Maybelle remembered. "She would stick to me like a leech. I thought of what would happen in an accident to June and I didn't ever get on that motorcyle again. But June was always like that. She was a gutsy little gal. Anita burned her ankle when she got on the Harley and wouldn't go near it again. But June loved it and cried when I told her she couldn't ride again."

The next day they traded in their motorcycles for a new Packard, which, in time, they used to travel down to Texas again. Doc had gone down there before their six-month vacation was over. He became interested in collecting songs in that area and rented a house in which he would live once their show began again.

In 1937 Eck could not get a leave of absence. Maybelle had to live alone in Texas with Anita. In the back of her mind, Maybelle was preparing to pass on her talent.

"It just seemed so natural," she remembered. "The children were always singing at home, and I looked at the joy I had singing for a living, and thought, why not teach the children a little of it too?" June and little Helen stayed with their Aunt Sylvia. But the way was clear for an expansion of the Carter Family.

# 9

# At the Crossroad

*They were at the crossroad. Having found themselves in a different America, they could not continue as a unit . . . . fit easily into the modern business of country music. Only Maybelle made the transition.*

The Carters were now radio professionals. They had achieved worldwide fame through their recordings, but their appearances thrust them into the mainstream of American culture. This period of influence was also a time of great personal sadness. Decision time had arrived for the Carter Family.

Their pace of broadcasting was not so difficult for them after their initial season. More and more transcriptions were being made, and they had more time to themselves. It was time they used to think about their personal situation. Doc and Sara worked well together in a professional capacity. Doc lived with Maybelle and Anita, in a small room in the back of their rented house in Del Rio. Sara lived by herself in a rented apartment. They would only meet to make transcriptions. Remarkably, the group continued to sing as well as ever. And variety was provided by the addition of a new voice. Anita Carter began to sing with them and occasionally had a solo number over the air. June Carter, at home with Aunt Sylvia, remembered her feelings at the time. "At night we listened to the powerful signal coming up from Texas, lying on our stomachs with our chins in our hands, me and Helen. Then Anita's voice would come over the air, and at first we didn't believe it was her. But Aunt Sylvia insisted, and it didn't seem right that Anita should be down in Texas with Mother, singing so well over the radio." The two children were extremely jealous and wrote their mother long letters begging her to let them come down. Finally Maybelle relented, telling them they could come to Texas and sing on the radio after her vacation.

Meanwhile Sara's life was changing. Coy Bayes came to Copper Creek during her second vacation from the radio station. Sara could see that he had come to court her, and indeed he asked her to marry him. That day she drove over to Maybelle's cabin with Coy to ask her friend to break the news to Doc.

Coy sounded his horn, and Maybelle came out on the

porch to greet them. On hearing the news, she hugged them both and promised to speak with Doc. Coy would be going back to California, Sara told her, and he would be getting a homestead ready for them in the year to come. Coy was a fine electrician and mechanic, as well as a good tree farmer, and he had good prospects back in the foothills of the Sierra Nevadas.

Doc wasn't at all upset, Maybelle remembered. She told him the news slowly, so he wouldn't get it all at once and be shocked. But he seemed to expect it and smiled when she finished telling him. He said it was the best thing for all concerned.

The year 1939 was to be the Carter Family's last one spent in Texas. Consolidated, unsure that station XERA would continue to broadcast through 1940, could not renew the Carters' contract. However, the sponsors were very satisfied with the group and raised each member's salary to the grand sum of $110 a week.

This was also the year Sara left Copper Creek for good. She and Coy were married in the early winter of 1939 in the Mount Vernon Methodist Church. Eck Carter was the best man, and Maybelle was the maid-of-honor. Doc Carter watched with a neutral expression from the back of the church.

The next day they all left for Texas. Their combined salaries amounted to a great deal of money in 1939, and the whole family could afford to come along. The road to Texas seemed an endless highway, June Carter remembered. As she looked at every piece of it flying by, she didn't want it to end. She had wanted so much to go down to Texas the year before, but when the time came, she wasn't so sure any more.

Two weeks before they left, Maybelle had been presented with a dilemma. Anita, the youngest, had been a proven favorite over XERA. Letters poured into the station praising her performances. Helen, the oldest, was also very capable of holding her own during a performance. She could sing, holding the highest notes, and could play a very adequate rhythm guitar.

June was another matter. "Doc came over to discuss how they would put the radio show together," June recalled, "and Mother called all of us children into the parlor. Doc nodded at Anita and Helen with approval. Then he turned to me. For a long time, everybody just stood and stared at me."

June remembered him shaking his head. "Maybelle," he said, "you have two weeks to work on her. Do your best."

Anita blew on a pitch pipe, and June tried to match it. She attempted to sing a melody, with Anita and Helen in perfect harmony behind her. Maybelle sat her down on the sofa, put an Autoharp in her lap, and placed a couple of picks on June's fingers. She was launched on her musical career.

For the next two weeks Maybelle, Anita, and Helen drilled her intensely. June learned quickly; she discovered a method of determining whether she was sharp or flat. She watched Maybelle and her sisters—all blessed with perfect pitch. When they winced June would adjust her tone! They soon realized this and began to aim their looks directly at June. "I learned twelve songs within two weeks," she remembered. "And I played the Autoharp without losing all the picks."

June was saying goodbye to her childhood. The mountains had been her only home—a world composed of gurgling streams, crawdads, and gravel-flippers. June cried a little as she was driven away from that most contented life. Her cousin Fern was her best friend, her "pal in the woods," who picked huckleberries with June on the slopes of Scott County. As they drove down the gravel road leading to the main highway, June clutched the gravel-flipper Fern had carved for her from an old dead tree.

"I was tiny," June remembered, "I was ten, and I was scared to leave the only home I had ever known." For ten-year-old "Junebug" Carter, the world was a huge, unknown territory. Past the mountains, past the rolling farmland of Tennessee, and Kentucky, approaching the Mississippi, the roads became straight. June remembered driving for miles and miles along a road as straight as a ribbon. Years later, June Carter recalled her impressions as a child. She felt sorrow for the people who lived on this land. Who had stolen their hills? There were no huckleberry patches, and the squirrels had nowhere to stow their acorns. What was even worse, there were no dogwood trees or tadpoles.

June sat in the backseat of the Packard with Autoharp picks on her fingers, a completely unhappy child. "I thought about jumping out of the car and running back to the Clinch Mountains, but a good pinch from Helen made me reconsider."

Maybelle and her children lived in San Antonio that winter. She rented rooms at Mrs. Murphy's boarding-house at 850 West Broadway. It was an exciting experience for the girls. They could run down the block and buy ice cream and penny candy at the corner drugstore. Sara boarded with them that year, while Coy Bayes prepared a home for her in California. Doc rented a house in Alamo Heights, where he lived with his children, Jeanette and Joe.

The Carter Family did no live broadcasts during their last year on XERA—all of their shows were transcribed. Don Baxter was the station's engineer, and the basement of his home became the center for their work in Texas during the next six months. Consolidated had expanded its activities to include other border-stations besides XERA, since Dr. Brinkley was now ill, and the future operation of the station was uncertain. The entire Carter Family show was now produced in the Baxter basement. Their new announcer, Bill Rinehard, urged the listeners to get their Kolor-Bak box tops in the mail. Those transcriptions were sent all over. Maybelle recalled. Stations XEG and XENT played them (besides XERA), and they were sent to fifty-thousand-watt stations all over the country. The Carters had never before enjoyed such a wide audience.

The original Carter Family sang less often as a trio now, because a new Carter grouping began to emerge. Doc, Sara, and Maybelle recorded two days a week, leaving the rest of the week's recording sessions to the children. On most of the programs featuring the Carter Family, Jeanette was added as a soloist. Two days a week were reserved for shows which would prominently feature Anita, Helen, and June.

June Carter recalled those sessions years later. "I tried to sing as low as I could. I didn't feel I could sing in tune yet, so I tried to have Anita and Helen drown me out." Maybelle gave the children a difficult assignment at their very first recording session. "We got to Don Baxter's house real early, and the three of us expected to see the Carter Family arrive to back us up instrumentally," June remembered. "But only mother arrived—without her guitar! We were expected to make all the music on our segment of the show!" June repeated history by singing "Engine 143" on that occasion. It was the perfect song for a ten-year-old. The song was four minutes long, and she kept on singing for all of it.

During this last Texas radio committment, Doc played less of a part in the group's performances. He had always had a habit of coming in and out of a song with the bass line—as the spirit moved him. He did this more and more. He liked to walk around the recording studio while the group recorded, and he would often walk out of the building in the middle of a song.

June Carter remembers Doc as a tall, taciturn man who was quite a mystery to the younger Carters. They used to visit him at his house—he was a fine whittler and would often fashion toys for them. But he would hardly say a word. When the children entered his house, they would often see him staring out the window at the unbroken Texas horizon.

Two months into their last Texas engagement, Coy Bayes got a job in the area. He and Sara moved into a rented house for the duration of the Carter Family contract. Coy was a great favorite with Maybelle's children. June in particular loved him. She thought him a giant. "He was six-feet-four and knew everything," June recalled. "One morning he told me to drink a large glass of hot water the minute I got out of bed. He said it would be good for me. So, almost every morning of our stay in Texas, I would drink a glass of hot water and run around the block. I didn't feel any healthier, as I remember, but it made me feel good to follow Uncle Coy's advice. I knew Aunt Sara was very lucky."

There is no way of knowing when the Carter Family first began considering a breakup. Their last year in Texas was not especially pleasant for any of them. Doc had practically corralled them into the group when they first began, but toward the end he might as well not have been in the group at all. He began to stay in the background during their recording sessions. For the first time in the history of the group, Doc avoided making decisions about what songs to perform over the air. It just developed that Maybelle and Sara suggested the songs, and he would nod his head. He'd look ahead with blank eyes like he was off somewhere else.

Doc Carter was always an unobtrusive presence on records, letting the abundant talents of Sara and Maybelle highlight almost every one of the group's selections. Now Doc rarely sang with the group and began to absent himself regularly from the sessions in the Baxter basement. He became involved in the activities of a local Methodist Church in San Antonio, organizing and directing a choir. Maybelle remembered visiting the church one Sunday and watching Doc work with the singers. She was surprised to hear them singing "God Gave Noah the Rainbow Sign." Without telling the other members of the group, Doc had arranged the song (which they had recorded in the early thirties) for a full chorus, and was conducting the chorus in rehearsal.

Maybelle then realized that Doc had decided to commit his life to Jesus Christ. She could not understand how it had escaped her attention before; but it was now obvious, and a likely explanation for Doc's recent behavior. As the choir sang out Doc flashed

Maybelle a bright smile. She went home and stopped worrying about him. Doc wasn't sick or depressed after all—his mind was on higher things.

In January 1940 the group left Texas. Sara and Coy Bayes moved into their homestead in Angel's Camp, California, and the rest of the Carters traveled back to the mountains. The group had not officially disbanded, but the strong familial bonds which had held the Carters so tightly were beginning to dissolve. Sara remained apart from all aspects of professional show business for the next year. Doc also ceased performing and devoted most of his time to the affairs of his beloved Mount Vernon Methodist Church.

Only Maybelle and her children persisted. Eck was back working on the railroad, and Maybelle could get free passes. This made touring around Virginia and Tennessee less difficult, and Maybelle went right back to touring when she returned to Scott County. But she did not disrupt her daughters' homelife in any way, enrolling them in the Hiltons school, and confining her performances to the weekends. The children were enlisted in these appearances and their musical education was continued.

"I became a performer then," June remembered. "The radio was easy for a child, just singing and playing in front of your family and the microphone. But now we had to play in front of strangers, and at first I was scared."

They played high schools and church suppers; sometimes they stopped at the coal fields to entertain weary men who needed recreation after a week of soul-destroying work. Money was scarce for the miners, and Maybelle and her children often took script instead of hard cash. (Script could only be spent in certain mining stores.) They weren't playing for money. By that time, singing was in Maybelle's blood—she just couldn't sit around without keeping at it.

Her children were the beneficiaries. After a few months of inactivity, Doc Carter began performing with them again. Maybelle convinced him to join her, because she sensed that Doc had to perform professionally, at least once in awhile, if he were to remain happy. It was for the children too, she told him, because he had so much to teach them. "I told him I had taught them as much as I could," she remembered, "and I guess it convinced him."

Anita and Helen became more accomplished, but June reaped the greatest benefit. At first she was shy and ill-at-ease; Doc and Maybelle handled her gently. They recognized a magnetism in June, the youngster had a saucy impertinence on stage, and audiences loved her. Doc urged June to introduce the first bits of comedy into a Carter Family performance. She would drag a big, wooden board across the stage. Maybelle or Doc asked where she was going, and June replied, "I'm looking for a room, I've got my board."

Early in 1941 Consolidated wrote Doc a letter asking if the original Family would consider doing a six-month stint on WBT, a radio station in Charlotte, North Carolina. It so happened that Sara Bayes was back east visiting, and the three original members sat down to make a decision. The company had made a most generous offer. Consolidated would pay them each $150 per week, plus a royalty based on the number of Kolor-Bak box tops listeners sent in—in response to their program.

Both Maybelle and Doc were eager to agree, but they expected Sara to object to the deal. They were surprised when she approved. She and Coy had spent a lot of money getting their homestead together, and the salary was too good to turn down.

Unlike their last stint in Texas, the Carters were required to perform in person. The contract specified that they do two shows daily from Monday through Friday, and one show on Saturday. In some ways the work was much harder. Doc was responsible for producing an hour and fifteen minutes of programming per day. He had to begin arranging material again and "working it up" so the Carter Family could sing it.

For the rest of the Carters, the radio stint at WBT was more pleasant than their Texas experience. Sara and Coy were quite happy living in a rented apartment, while they earned the money to build up their homestead. Eck Carter was working as a mail clerk on the Southern Railway, and was able to live with Maybelle in Charlotte. (That city was one of the stops on his run.)

Their children could go to school every day and still participate in the Saturday-night radio program.

"We all got on well at the station," Maybelle remembered. "But it still seemed more and more like a job, not like the old times." The Carter Family was becoming less and less a family, and more a purely professional organization. This bothered Maybelle Carter.

"I loved performing for the sake of it all," she recollected. "I would have gone on WBT by myself. But when you sing with people you've known all your life, you can't help having all the memories flooding over you some of the time." But everything was put aside when the "on the air" sign flashed on. One might expect the Carters to let their feelings get in the way of their music, but it never happened. They were calm and collected when they performed. When it was time to make music, they followed through with such class and presence it was hard to believe.

Other aspects of this radio engagement bothered the Carters. There were many Carter children in 1941, and the operation of the group was becoming cumbersome. Doc had the production responsibilities, and he began to find it difficult to accommodate all the members of the group. At that time, the children were naturally jealous of each other, and Doc was forced to bruise many an ego in allocating the limited air-time. "Sometimes the racket," Maybelle recalls, "was deafening. There were times when we didn't let any of the children sing on the air, there were so many arguments. And Doc took the brunt of it."

For Maybelle, however, the increased size of the family was a small factor in the rising tension they all felt. Splitting up was on everybody's mind when the contract was about to run out. It hardly seemed worthwhile to spend time together, when it was plainly so uncomfortable, especially for Sara and Doc. Consolidated was anxious for them to sign another contract as audience response surpassed all expectations. They wanted the Carters to stay as long as their popularity lasted.

When their contract expired, however, the Carters had no desire to continue. Sara and Coy had accumulated more than enough money to establish their homestead in California and were anxious to begin their journey west. Doc was tired—he had never worked so hard at music in his life—and it was not fun for him anymore. Everybody around the station commented on how drawn and tired he looked.

Only Maybelle still had the desire to perform. She wanted her daughters to experience all aspects of the music business. She wanted to teach her daughters all she knew, and they wanted to learn. After WBT, she looked forward to singing on the stage with her daughters. Eck wanted it as much as she did.

They were at the crossroad. Having found themselves in a different America, they could not continue as a unit. Twenty years later Doc Carter was in a thoughtful mood when he recalled how he always felt out-of-place working on the radio, especially on WBT. It was a real modern layout, and it covered practically all of the southeast, but he was more nervous talking through those microphones than he ever was before people.

For Doc Carter, a radio-control room was not the proper place to make music. "I'd stand there nervous for an hour before a show, going over the songs in my mind. I'd look at all those meters and dials and try not to let them bother me, but I never could forget them. All the jumping needles and flashing lights would always make me jittery. It just wasn't the same over radio. I loved to sing before folks, because I could see their faces, and see their toes tapping when they really like a song. Singing on the radio was like singing against a blank wall. You never knew how the people liked your singing."

Maybelle had made the transition to radio more easily. At first she had felt guilty about bringing her children to Texas, then on tours, and finally on WBT. In the mountains children always worked with their parents, but the work in Scott County was rural work. The children could remain at home, get as much schooling as possible, and make friends among the children of the surrounding valleys. Her children's musical work, however, separated them from their own age group, and in most ways tended to make Anita, Helen, and June outsiders. Now Maybelle was proud of her children's talents and the education which travel provided for them, but she still worried about the life she was thrusting upon them. How could they avoid growing up too fast in the hothouse atmosphere of show business? It was a danger Maybelle had to guard against.

June had developed into quite a tomboy. After their stint on WBT ended, she took to driving a tar truck down the narrow mountain roads just to show the men of the valley that she could drive as well as a man. Maybelle remembered giving her quite a licking one day when she ran into the house with her overalls coated with tar.

But her children were adaptable, and the distortions in their behavior caused by the family career were minor, and easily corrected. Eck and Maybelle both decided to spend at least six months in Scott County after the WBT contract expired. There the children could attend a school in their native valley, and begin to live a normal life again. Doc moved back to his cabin in Maces Spring, and established a general store at the crossroads, where he spent his time reminiscing and singing with friends and neighbors. For the moment they left the music business to the new, and polished professionals who were now on top.

The visit of a *Life Magazine* reporter and photographer was a reminder of their fame. They came unexpectedly in late September 1941. They asked about the family and wanted to know where Sara and Doc were. Doc was on a trip out of the county, and Sara and Coy Bayes were in California. June remembered, "They had to make do with us, and they were even more surprised when we told them the Carter Family had broken up, and Maybelle Carter was the only one left performing."

In the end, however, the reporters were satisfied and began photographing Maybelle, Eck, and the children for a picture story in *Life*. But fate, in the form of December 7, 1941, intervened. *Life Magazine* became preoccupied with Pearl Harbor, and news pertaining to World War II took precedence over the Carter Family story. Young June Carter kept the scene in her mind. The photographer had taken many pictures, and June treasured a bushel basket full of burnt flashbulbs for months afterward.

# 10

# Anchored in Love

*"We felt the presence of the Lord there.". . . . Before the congregation, they humbly accepted Jesus Christ as their personal Saviour.*

It was obvious to Eck Carter that his wife needed time to recuperate from the ordeals of her professional career. Eck also believed the children needed a respite from the rigors of the music business. Helen, the oldest, was fifteen, and both Maybelle and Eck wanted her to finish high school. Neither of them had gotten that far in their education.

Maybelle agreed to suspend her career for an indefinite time. This vacation was to be her last for almost twenty-five years. Although she must have needed the rest after the hectic radio work over WBT, Maybelle was restless. She gardened, helped Eck with chores around the homestead, and did charity work with Doc for the Mount Vernon Methodist Church. But performing still lured her. After three months she began to seem withdrawn, and acted a bit testy, as though not singing for people didn't suit her at all. The Carter girls were on her side; they loved going around and singing, and wanted to get their mother to sing again.

But Eck Carter was adamant. "I don't want you to wear yourself down," he told his wife. "We have enough money, so you can afford to rest." Eck was not an unobservant husband, however. He knew of Maybelle's love for music, and had set a time limit for her enforced vacation. After six months had gone by, he walked up to his wife while she was tending the garden. "I can't stand seeing your long face any more," he told her, according to Helen. "Go out and find someplace to sing."

He was joking, of course. Offers had been pouring into their mountain homestead ever since the job at WBT had ended. At first the most difficult task for Maybelle was to pick and choose among the many attractive job offers.

It finally came down to a choice between the offers made by sponsors and radio stations. Maybelle did not want to uproot her family again, but Eck, as always, was completely understanding. "If the money is good, take it," he told her. "The mountains will always be here."

Luckily, however, the most attractive offer came from a station in Richmond, Virginia. The station wanted them to appear once a week on a barn-dance program. Maybelle had only to travel across the state with her daughters. Their lives would not be disrupted at all, and each of the children would receive a good salary, which they could bank toward their education.

In this way Maybelle Carter's post-Family career began. They signed an eighteen-month contract on WRVA's "Old Dominion Barn Dance." At first the pace was much slower than it had been on their other radio stints. It was only once a week, and they were only on for five or ten minutes of a two-hour program. The salaries were as high as they had been on WBT.

On WRVA Maybelle and her daughters sang the songs made popular by the original Carter Family. June, however, soon became especially popular with the audience, and the fourteen-year-old girl became something of a comedienne, bantering between songs with Maybelle or the announcer. The gales of laughter from the studio audience soon led to an expansion of the Carter's segment on the Barn Dance.

The response to their appearances led to a resurgence of touring. Eck Carter began to work part-time as his wife's manager, booking appearances throughout the southeast. Maybelle was always worried about the way he felt, Eck remembered. She thought her singing would make him jealous, or something like that—but it never did. After an eighteen-month stint on WRVA, Maybelle and her daughters immediately began their own thirty-minute program over WNOX, in Knoxville, Tennessee. At this time, Eck Carter quit his job with the railroad to work full-time as tour manager for his wife and daughters.

The demand for their services increased. For the first time in her professional career, Maybelle began to tour across the country on a regular basis. Their group was now known as the "Carter Sisters," and during their tours they were beginning to lay the foundations of a new popularity. It was unquestionably the hardest work Maybelle and her children had ever done. They purchased a new Packard and drove it hard, playing cities as far away from Maces Spring as Bakersfield, California. Helen, Anita, and June had left any vestige of a normal life far behind as their show business careers gathered momentum.

The new group did not primarily rely on the material of the original Carter Family. Maybelle began to write more songs, and the group sang these, as well as their own versions of country music standards.

By the late forties the Carter Sisters were well-known throughout the country. The group began to reach a wide audience over Si Siman's station KWTO, in Springfield, Missouri. At this time, June Carter blossomed, and the outlines of her individual career began to emerge. In 1949 she made the top-ten with her parody rendition of "Baby, It's Cold Outside," which she recorded with Homer and Jethro. Maybelle was proud of June then, and recalled how she had always been independent. She remembered June driving that tar truck down the mountain roads on a bet, just to show she could drive as well as a man.

In the early fifties the Carter Sisters and Maybelle joined the "Grand Ole Opry," the mecca of country music (broadcast over WSM in Nashville, Tennessee). They signed record contracts with Columbia and Decca at this time. Among their hits were "Amazing Grace," "Wabash Cannonball," "Are You Afraid to Remember Me," and "Blood That Stained the Old Rugged Cross."

The Carter Sisters were soon to go out touring on their own, with Maybelle staying behind at the Opry. The thought of the grind of touring dissuaded her, and she chose to continue on the radio show once a week. She also limited her tours to the immediate area surrounding her new home in Nashville.

June Carter, in the meantime, was broadening her career. She continued to appear on the Grand Ole Opry with her mother and sisters until 1954, but a large part of her time was devoted to her growing interest in dramatics. In that year she quit the Opry and moved to New York. There she attended the Actors' Studio, and was able to land dramatic parts on television. In the late fifties she appeared on "Jim Bowie" and "Gunsmoke," and her performances won her accolades.

She did not abandon her music. June struck out on her own as a singer, and guested on shows hosted by Tennessee Ernie Ford, Jack Paar, and Garry Moore. In the mid-fifties she signed an individual recording contract with Columbia. "Tennessee Mambo," and "Love, Oh, Crazy Love" were among her hits during this time. By 1960 June Carter was coming into her prime as a country-music performer. The competition was still intense, but she had been seasoned, and was well known throughout the industry. She began to write songs, and was almost immediately successful. Several of her songs were recorded by country-music stars, and eventually made the top-ten.

In 1961 Johnny Cash, who seemed destined for the summit of his profession, asked her to join his touring troupe. In the early fifties Maybelle and the Carter Sisters had toured for a short time with Elvis Presley, and it was Presley who suggested that Cash hire June for his act. She came highly recommended. At first there was a question about accepting the offer. Her own singing and writing career was just taking off. Some people told her that her career might suffer; they said to keep going on her own. But June had other ideas. She felt she could really develop with the Cash troupe; she would be writing songs for one of the biggest stars in the business and singing on the stage with Johnny and his fine backup musicians. That was enough for her!

June Carter's career did not suffer in the least. In 1962 she signed an exclusive five-year personal-appearance contract with Cash. She also began writing songs with him. In 1963 they coauthored "The Matador," which became one of Johnny's major hits. June also teamed up with other fine songwriters. In the same year she coauthored "Ring of Fire" with Merle Kilgore—a song which skyrocketed to number one on the charts when Cash recorded it. This song became a country-music classic. In professional combination, Johnny and June seemed to have a special magic. Their tours were fabulously successful, and by 1968 they had become a part-time singing team. In 1967 they produced two big country-music hits "Jackson" and "Guitar Pickin' Man."

These triumphs took their toll on Johnny Cash. He had become a star overnight in the fifties, and he had found it difficult to adjust to his success. By the time June Carter joined his troupe, Cash was estranged from his wife and was using amphetamines. His behavior became extremely erratic. However, during his up-periods there was no one in the country-music business who could match the fertility of his musical gift.

When June first joined the troupe, she immediately sensed that something was wrong. The members of the troupe were fond of practical jokes, and played many on June in the first months of her association with the entourage. They were harmless enough, and June did not take them seriously. But she witnessed some destructive episodes herself, and heard rumors of others. Information was easy to come by in the close-knit world of country music, and June soon found out that Cash was addicted.

The course of action she followed after learning this fact is a tribute to her Christian charity. She told Maybelle Carter of Cash's troubles and asked her mother for advice. Maybelle was puzzled at first. She couldn't understand why June was so concerned about the problem. But then she began to realize that June was in love with Johnny. Maybelle decided to help in any way she could. Maybelle and Eck invited Cash to spend time at their place outside Nashville whenever he felt like resting and getting away from the hectic pace of his professional schedule. But that seemed to have little effect. Even though the Carters gave Cash a temporary refuge, the pressures of his career were driving him deeper into addiction.

It was now obvious to everyone that June and Johnny were in love. He had divorced his wife a year earlier, and the way was open for a marriage, but June held back. Cash's life was in disarray; and, although she cared for him deeply, June could not marry him until his addiction was conquered. Johnny was now locked into the familiar pattern common to so many country-music stars. He was burning himself out like a roman candle, and nobody could force him to slow down. It was a decision only he alone could make. Fortunately for country music, Johnny Cash made that decision. Taking June's sound advice he agreed to seek medical help.

Johnny's doctor wasn't optimistic. He knew how high the odds were against his being able to lick the addiction. But Johnny Cash now knew he would have to conquer it, or surrender his life. Maybelle, June, and the doctor were in constant attendance. There was no other way for him to fight the pills. He needed their steady advice, love, and encouragement.

June Carter worked the hardest. For two very anxious weeks, Cash was made an invalid. Even though he was strong enough physically to leave his mansion, the doctor would not allow it. The amphetamines were the easiest drug habit to kick for Cash. The tranquilizer habit, which he had also built up, caused him agony during that time, particularly when he suffered hallucinations. It was at those times that June took him in her arms, and comforted him. Gradually he recovered.

After almost two months of enforced idleness, Cash felt that he had succeeded in his struggles over drugs. The doctor verified that Johnny was physically free of the addiction, but counseled him to be very careful. The psychological conditions which led to drug abuse would still be there—the career pressures, and the urge to drive himself relentlessly. Life has to be filled with supports one can depend upon. What those will be is up to the individual. Cash already knew what they were to be for him.

After staying off pills for six months, he secretly proposed to June Carter. They made an agreement. If Cash could be drug-free for another six months, they would set a wedding date.

They were married on the first of March, 1968, in a little Methodist church in Franklin, Kentucky. Merle Kilgore, the coauthor of "Ring of Fire," was the best man. Cash had found one support. June Carter Cash loved Johnny with a stern love, and she watched him vigilantly for signs of tension, the tension which would drive him back to pills.

And the pressures mounted after Johnny's marriage, as the doctor had predicted. Pills were a constant temptation. June's love, however, helped him hold the line during these difficult times. But Cash could not have made it with her alone. At her urging he began to read the Bible, and in 1971, at Evangel Temple in Nashville, he gave his life to Jesus Christ. They had been to churches all over the Nashville area trying to find a place where they could find God. "We felt the presence of the Lord there," June testified. "Johnny would come out of that church with a gleam in his eye, and a glow on his face. The more we went to Evangel Temple, the calmer and more serene Johnny became. It made me very happy." On that day in May, then, June and Johnny quietly left their pews and knelt before the altar. Before the congregation, they humbly accepted Jesus Christ as their personal Saviour.

In 1970 June Carter Cash gave birth to a son, and they gave him a name which predicted the continuance of a musical family. John Carter Cash made evident their faith in God, and in the future.

"Isn't it wonderful?" Maybelle Carter asked. "That child will someday realize how lucky he is. He's half Cash and half Carter. In country music that just can't be beaten."

John Carter Cash was their anchor in love, the foundation of a marriage which had resurrected the Lazarus of country music, Mr. Johnny Cash.

# 11

# Country Music Hall of Fame

*"I put my life in the Lord's hands early, and He has never let me down."*

They had come together again. On this day in October, 1970, Maybelle and Sara Carter were to be inducted into the Country Music Hall of Fame here in Nashville, Tennessee. They had not been on a stage, together, for almost thirty years (although they did make a Columbia album in the mid-sixties called *Historic Reunion*). The years had flown by. The crowd beyond the drawn curtain was packed into the Ryman Auditorium. Maybelle and Sara heard its murmurings. Maybelle had been on this stage many times before, as one of the stars of the

"Grand Ole Opry," but Sara had never been in Ryman Auditorium. Both of them were as nervous as the greenest show-business beginner.

Outside the auditorium, the crowds had gathered early. It was a Friday night in Nashville, and normally the Ryman Auditorium would be closed. But that night the streets around Broadway and Opry Place were alive. The arc lights made the air seem to hang above the crowd. Thousands of headlights flared the lenses of the TV news cameras, yellowing the faces of bystanders who lined the curbs. They peered into the darkened limousines, hoping for a glimpse of a star on his way to the ceremony.

The crowds lined the alleys behind the auditorium, hoping that standing room would still be available when it was their turn to walk through the swinging front doors. Linebaugh's Restaurant ("Where the Opry Stars Meet to Eat") was filled with patrons who had given up hope. There was no way anyone could get into Ryman tonight. Instead, they pressed their faces up against the plate-glass windows, murmuring every time a silvery limousine pulled up to the kleig lights and TV cameras in front of the Opry House.

Maybelle had no real conception of the scene outside. In her forty-three years in show business, she had never been outside the Opry just before a show. When she was in town, Maybelle Carter would be on the stage, preparing to perform. But she could understand the kind of excitement which was generated by an expectant Opry crowd.

This night was unusual because there was excitement on both sides of the stage. Usually backstage is crowded with performers; but the mood is one of nonchalance, as though the place were filled with workers on a coffee break. But tonight was different. Everybody milled around, as if they did not know what to say or where to stand. They left Maybelle and Sara standing alone, giving them privacy on the biggest night of their career.

Tonight, the Country Music Association was honoring the pioneers of country music by installing them as charter members in the Country Music Hall of Fame. Jimmie Rodgers and A. P. Carter were to be honored posthumously. The climax of the show belonged to Maybelle and Sara, along with members of the Johnny Cash troupe, who would accompany them. But all the attention, and all the pressure, would be on Maybelle and Sara.

Time seemed to accelerate. Maybelle and Sara had their make-up applied, cue sheets were handed over, and camera position and stand-lines were described. Then the amber lights winked on, making the TV cameras look like one-eyed monsters giving them a baleful stare. The technicians, all wearing earphones, crouched behind their machines. Microphone booms swung over their heads. By this time Sara was more nervous than Maybelle. "You've always been the trouper," she had told Maybelle the night before. "You'll make it fine. It's me I'm worried about."

Maybelle had certainly been the trouper of the group, enjoying the music business even more than Doc, who did not especially enjoy the day-to-day routine of the business aspects of it. It had been Maybelle who kept right on performing after the original group split up—who trained her own daughters into successful performers in their own right. It was Maybelle who most deserved to be known as "the Queen Mother of Country Music."

Sara had retired in the early forties, and had spent the following years in happiness with her husband, Coy Bayes. Church work filled up most of her days, and she was now more at home raising funds for church projects than she was singing at the "Grand Ole Opry." This was something entirely new for both of them, transcending anything they had ever experienced before. As a professional, Maybelle could forge ahead, counting on their talent to pull them through. Sara could still sing as well as ever, and the audience would be more than satisfied with that.

They had memorized the ceremony, and Maybelle ran over it in her mind as the glittering curtain suddenly went up. The audience stood and applauded even before the curtain had risen an inch off the stage. The waves of sound thundered toward them and they were both momentarily overwhelmed. The cameras moved toward them. Technicians pointed in the air. Then, the orchestra began to play, and the welcome began to subside. "Ladies and Gentlemen," said the announcer. "Welcome to the 'Grand Ole Opry.' This is a very special night. We're here to honor our roots. In this business, some of us tend to forget our history. But tonight, we have two of the finest musicians country music has to offer. I give you Maybelle Addington Carter, and Sara Dougherty Carter!"

Ryman Auditorium exploded. The standing ovation resumed. Technicians were applauding and smiling. Sara and Maybelle were alone on that big stage, receiving love and respect from people who had admired their music for over four decades.

After five minutes the applause ended; Sara began strumming the Autoharp, and Maybelle began picking out "The Wildwood Flower." When Sara began to sing in her clear, penetrating voice, the applause briefly began again. Maybelle hoped the TV cameras could not pick up her tears. It was all she could do to keep picking out the classic melody. Her emotions were almost overwhelming her. They finished singing, and the ceremonies began.

Johnny Cash stepped out and told the story of Doc Carter's life. "Doc Carter died peacefully in his sleep on the morning of November 7, 1960, having spent the years since 1942 in peaceful retirement," Cash summed up. "He was buried in the cemetery of his beloved Mount Vernon Methodist Church in Maces Spring. I remember the time I visited the church. Having never heard a description of his monument nor mention of it, I walked around and read, A. P. CARTER. No date, no flowering verse, but just under that name was imbedded a gold record, which stated Doc Carter's appropriate words simply and boldly: KEEP ON THE SUNNY SIDE."

Johnny Cash then hugged them both, and stood behind them on the stage. It was like the TV show "This Is Your Life," Sara remembered thinking at the time. June Carter Cash appeared next. "I'll never forget," she told the audience, "the night at the 'Grand Ole Opry' when my mother forgot the words to 'Wildwood Flower.' " The audience roared out a laugh.

Don Howard, their boss at XERA, came out to say a few words, as did Harry Steele, their old announcer. Roy Acuff spoke about his days with Maybelle at the "Grand Ole Opry," and other people came up to pay their respects—people who had been with them at different stages of their careers.

Johnny Cash stepped up to the microphone again, and the auditorium fell into a hushed quiet. "It's time to do homage, friends," he said in a quiet voice. A stage assistant handed him two golden plaques. Cash held them, and the light from the spots flashed off their surfaces. "I am proud to acknowledge a debt to two most upright women, Sara and Maybelle, members of the original Carter Family, who started all of us youngsters on our way."

The audience roared again as Maybelle and Sara stepped forward to receive their plaques. As they stood for a moment, bathed in the adulation of the crowd, a stagehand gave Cash another plaque. He raised his hand for the crowd to be quiet, and they obeyed him almost at once.

"I never knew Doc Carter," Cash said, "but I know his music. He discovered and wrote more than 300 songs, songs which form the foundation of my music and yours." Cash glanced back at Sara and Maybelle, and he could clearly see their tears. "Maybelle, Sara, would you accept this plaque, inducting A. P. Carter into the Country Music Hall of Fame?"

They both walked forward unsteadily. Maybelle held out her hands and received the plaque. She could not believe the fanciness of the lettering, the heft of this object of mahogany, silver, and gold. Now one of them would have to say a few words.

This was the most frightening moment of all. Both Sara and Maybelle were overwhelmed. How could they express their thanks for a moment which comes to few people in this life? Maybelle had promised to speak for both of them when they received their honor, and she could not refuse to do so now. Cradling the plaques in one arm, she gripped the microphone stand uncertainly. She could see Coy Bayes sitting in the front row, clapping and shouting encouragement. Eck Carter sat next to him, a prideful smile on his face. Maybelle looked at her plaque for a moment before looking out at the audience again.

"If you told me forty-three years ago that I'd be standing here I wouldn't have believed you. But this is where my life has led. Believe me, I don't take the credit. Sara here was our voice. Without Doc's pushing, we wouldn't have made it far at all, and neither would Sara." Maybelle paused. Her knees felt a bit unsteady for a moment, and when she glanced at Eck down in the audience tears flowed into her eyes again. Sara reached over and squeezed her hand.

"But it wasn't really any of our doing," she continued, "I put my life in the Lord's hands early, and He has never let me down." The vast audience packing the Ryman Auditorium fell silent for a moment, silenced by the force of spoken truth. Then the moment passed, and the audience's roar of approval filled the hall.

The Carter Family was on stage again, and they belonged to them all.